STROMATA THEOLOGICA, HISTORICA, &

PROPHETICA;

OR,

Theological, Historical, and Prophetical Pieces

OF

PATCHWORK:

FOR THE

AMUSEMENT OF THE CURIOUS, INSTRUCTION OF

THE IGNORANT, AND BENEFIT OF ALL.

said to be written by Steel
Dickson a presbyterian
Minister   PATCH I. *in the County of*
Ireland.— who was arrested in
1798 on suspicion of being concerned
in the Rebellion. LONDON:
PRINTED FOR THE BOOKSELLERS.

1805.

TO J. L——, PRINTER, LONDON.

MY DEAR FRIEND,

IN my late private residence, in the lower parts of Germany, for certain purposes, unnecessary to be mentioned, I found it necessary to assume a variety of characters. That of a politician was out of the question. Philosophy would serve no purpose, as the name is unattended to, amidst the tumults of war. Devotion, however, keeps pace with its terrors, dangers, and alarms: and, when unguided by knowledge, gives itself up to the delusions of fancy, either superstitious or enthusiastic.

The prevalent cast in many places of the continent, particularly among those of the lower order, induced me to give in to these prejudices, and to yield a pretended assent to all their legends, visions, and prophecies. This accommodating temper recommended me irresistibly to an old priest, in a little village, near Petersburgh. He was good-humoured, credulous, and ignorant. He told me that his family had come from the borders of the Euxine sea ; that he did not perfectly know the time of their removal, as, in the various revolutions, which they had undergone, every line of writing had been lost, except a tattered manuscript, partly in the Sclavonian language, and partly in Latin ; that it was in some parts historical ; in others, theological ; and in a few, prophetical : and, that he was sure, it was written by one of his ancestors.

This, you may be certain, fired my curiosity, and determined me, if possible, to see this wondrous manuscript. My good old friend gratified me ; but, alas ! the character in which it was written, rendered it, to me, totally useless. However, his good nature soon relieved me. On seeing my embarrassment, he immediately offered to translate it into German, or give me a copy of the whole in Latin. The offer delighted me. The glowing benignity with which it was made, did more— it rivetted my heart to his in bonds of friendship.

The next day, he said, he was obliged to be abroad, *on duty*, for a few weeks, and professed his regret, on leaving me: but hoped the pleasure of meeting again would compensate the pain of a separation so short,

On the fourteenth or fifteenth day afterwards, he met me with all the appearance of being just returned from a journey. He dined with me. But, what was my surprise, when, after dinner, he presented me with a roll, saying; " Here, my friend, is what I promised you: I hope God will give you grace to make a *proper use* of it. On a few occasions, I have thrown out some doubts and queries. May God of his infinite grace, give you wisdom to resolve them fully and clearly, for the illumination, regeneration, and sublimation of the souls of men."

Both the matter, and manner of his address affected me. The roll was, partly a copy, and partly a translation, of the manuscript in question, in travelling over which, his fourteen days had been employed. On looking over it, I found some extravagancies, several shrewd queries, and a few bold (I might say, wild) conjectures. However, with all its peculiarities, it contains a great portion of good sense. Such as it is, I send you my version of my friend's translation. From his peculiarities, and the *mongrelism* of his Latin, I fear I have not always done him justice. However, as I have not willingly misrepresented, I know his shade (the good man died 15 months ago) looks down on me with complacence. Such as the performance is, I gladly present it to you, knowing you will give it fairly to the world. I have ventured to add a few remarks of my own, mostly *corrective*. Dispose of them as your own sound judgment shall direct, and be assured of the most profound consideration of,

Sir,

Your very humble servant, &c. &c.

May 28th, 1804.

TO THE PUBLIC.

HAVING read the preceding letter, I proceeded to peruse the papers sent me, of which the following sheets contain the first part. Ye will find that, with all their peculiarities, they contain much good sense, and a large mass of ecclesiastical matter, compressed into small bounds. Convinced that their contents may be, not only amusing to the curious, but instructive to the young, and others unversed in ecclesiastical history, and who have not access to more copious records, I humbly present this first part to your discerning eye. Should it meet with that favorable reception, which I hope, and to which I think it justly entitled, I shall, at a future day, take the liberty of submitting the remainder to your perusal. With warmest wishes for the extension of useful knowledge, and the interests of pure religion and morality, I am,

&c. &c.

THE EDITOR.

LONDON, MAY 10TH, 1805.

BEING early convinced of the truth of the Christian Revelation, and captivated with its meek, candid, and benevolent spirit, and the amiable character of its first professors, my youthful heart glowed with the enchanting thought, that, wherever it spread, it would be productive of the same candor, meekness, and benevolence in all who received it. Looking around me, in the circle of my acquaintance, all of whom professed to be Christians, the ardor of my heart was immediately chilled by the instances of meanness, falshood, fraud, debauchery, impiety, and cruelty, which every where presented themselves. "Father of light, life, and love," exclaimed I, " can these be, in sincerity and truth, the disciples of the blessed Jesus ? No! they cannot be taught of Him, else they would have imbibed his spirit, and walked in his ways. Yet, they *all* call *themselves his* disciples, and *thy* children. Whence can this inconsistency have proceeded ? At what time did it take its rise ? By what means did it grow up ? When was it completed ?"

Shocked at the inconsistency, and burning with the desire of accounting for it, I exclaimed again, " I must —I will—be satisfied. History—the remembrance-book of ages, will resolve all my questions, and remove my every doubt. To history I will fly."

This determination, in some measure, relieved me. I considered my object as half-attained. However, a new difficulty soon presented itself. Of the few books I possessed, history made no portion, except the historical part of the Bible ; and, I knew, it did not come down to these latter times, except by " it's sure word of prophesy." While my mind was thus employed, I was called upon by a monk, belonging to a convent, some miles distant. His face was to me " as the face of an angel of God." The library of his convent presented itself to my imagination. " Welcome, my friend," said I. " Never was reviving cordial more welcome to the fainting spirit, than thy presence is to me." I embraced him with ardor. He looked amazed. " The library of your convent," said I, more composed, " is reported to be very extensive. I presume it contains all the best histories of the christian church." " Yes," said he, still looking surprised, " and of the world." " I wish to read church history," replied I. " Do you think your Prior would indulge me with the use of such authors as I may want?" " Of that I have no doubt;" rejoined he. " Our Prior is a good man, and esteems you. But why"——" No questions now," said I, laying my hand on his breast. " In due time your curiosity shall be satisfied." The truth is, I was afraid of his questions; for, though not illiberal, *as times are*, I was not sure he would have approved of my motives. After some conversation, he took a refreshment, and left me, with a promise that he would apply to the Prior, in my behalf, and let me know the result.

He had scarcely left me, till the idea of the Bible, again, came across my mind. I determined to read it, with more than usual attention, particularly, where it might glance at the subject which now engrossed my every thought. I recollected that the Jewish people were stubborn, ungrateful, and disobedient ; and that their conduct was, frequently, irreconcileable to the principles of their religion. " I will read their records," resolved I. " They will, *surely*, furnish me with many facts—*perhaps*, with means of accounting for them. And, where these facts are similar to such as I find recorded in the books which I intend to read, (as men, in all ages, nearly resemble each other,) they may help me to account for them also. Besides, the Jewish scriptures have foretold the coming of Messiah ; prefigured his kingdom ; the means by which it shall be established ; the enemies which shall rise against it ; the revolutions it shall undergo ; the causes from which they shall proceed ; and many other things concerning it. Who can tell what light these may shed on the subjects of my inquiry—what aid to my judgment in forming its conclusions? With humble dependence on the Father of Light, I shall set out on my research. May his word be the light of my path, and his spirit my guide to the Oracle of Truth!"

In that calm composure, which the preceding apostrophe diffused over my whole soul, I opened the book of God. From the brief sketch of characters, events, revolutions, and catastrophes, previous to the giving of the law, little, to my purpose, attracted my attention. From that period, a people, a government, a religion, and a priesthood, present themselves to view. From the nature of the government; the simplicity, purity, and piety of the precepts, the arrangement of the services, and the solemn sanctions of religion as clothed with the authority of God; Virtue, personal, domestic, social, and civil, might be naturally expected to form the national character; and peace, comfort, and prosperity, it's uninterrupted portion. From the days of Moses, during the government of the judges (356 years,) few enormities appear in the conduct, either of governors, priests, or people; and these are but indistinctly marked. However, towards the end of that period, the two vices most destructive to a state, and degrading to a people, seem to have become prevalent—unbridled sensuality—and griping avarice. That these should have been generally prevalent, cannot be wondered at, when we read that the sons of Eli, the priest, openly abused the women, "at the door of the tabernacle, whither they came to worship;"* and that, about sixty years afterwards, the sons of Samuel, judge and prophet, "turned aside after gain, perverted judgment, and sold public offices for money."† The rapacity of the priesthood, patronised by the sons of Eli, already mentioned, is described in terms which excite indignation and horror. It was their custom, when any man offered sacrifice, to send their servants with three-pronged forks, which they struck into the pan, where the meat was boiled, and carried away all they could lift.‡ At other times, they demanded raw meat for the spit, with fat for basting; and, if refused, however discreetly, took it by force. The manner in which this is told by the sacred historian, is truly affecting.§

* I Sam. 2, 22. A. C. 1165. † 8, 13. ‡ See I Sam. § 2, 13, 14, 15, 16.

The effect of this licentiousness, and rapacity of the sons of Eli, was the ruin of his family.—That, of the vices of those of Samuel, a revolution in the government.

From this revolution, until the division of the nation into the kingdoms of Judah and Israel, we find no trait of national character, either moral or religious. A political one, indeed presented itself; yet it scarcely deserves the name. It is true, the change from a popular to a kingly government proceeded from the people. No political principle, however, was concerned in the business. The fact was simply this. They were weary of the sons of Samuel—They hated, and were determined to be rid of them. The little nations around them, were all governed by kings, and they were determined to be in the fashion. "Make us a king," say they to Samuel, "to judge us *like all the nations.*"* And, to Samuel's sensible remonstrance on the subject, they repeat with vehemence; "Nay, but we will have a *King* over us, that *we also may be like all the nations.*" This repeated declaration of a silly misguided people, tempts me to suspect that there is *fun*, as well as *fact*, in the account of the *Asses*. Kish, the father of Saul, is mentioned as a man of "power," or "wealth." Perhaps he might possess both, as the one generally leads to, or commands the other. The discontented state of the people could not be unknown to him; and, it is very likely, he might be disposed to take advantage of it. His son, Saul, was a fine sturdy fellow, taller, by the head and shoulders, than any man in the country. This was a lucky circumstance, when size and bodily strength were the chief recommendation to power, then principally military; and the people declared, that they wanted one "to go before them, and fight their battles."† The old man, knowing this, thought there would be no harm in throwing his son in their way. Any pretext would do. That of the *asses*, was as good as the best: nay, it seems better than any other, in the then besotted state of the public mind. The event proved it so. Saul was appointed king; and, immediately after, he is told, "*The asses which thou wentest to seek, are found.*"‡

* I. Sam. 8, 5, 20.   † I. Sam. 8, 20.   ‡ I. Sam. 10, 2.

It is further remarkable, that the asses were females. This may imply, that the men of Israel were become "effeminate," that is, weak as women, in body, and timid in mind. What gives strength to this is, that, in some antient plays, he who was taken prisoner, and condemned to be the slave of another, was called "*Onos*"* (Ass).

Be this as it may, the people are no more heard of, during the life of Saul, than his father's asses. The history of his reign is only a brief record of his follies, impertinences, presumptions, madness, cowardice, envy, malice, superstition, despondency, and suicide.

The history of David relates nothing but his wars, adultery, murders, concubinage, and death.

Nor does the history of the reign of Solomon cast any light on the moral or religious character of the Jewish people. The government had become absolute, the court pompous and profligate; and the people, reduced to slavery, scarcely appear, even in the back ground. The king himself, during a long reign, was a strange compound of wisdom and folly, devotion and impiety, prudence in words, and pomposity in actions. In licentiousness he was unrivalled. He abused himself with women of every nation, feature, and complexion. He collected wives to the number of seven hundred, and concubines to that of three;† and, unable to gratify their wanton wishes, he indulged their wild superstitions, by introducing their gods, building them temples, and sanctioning their worship.

While the king was thus wallowing in sensuality, and enslaved by superstition, it could not be supposed that either his family or his subjects, should be much impressed with sentiments of morality or religion. Such an example must have tended to eradicate all sense of both, to extinguish virtuous sensibility, overwhelm principle, and reduce national character to meanness and depravity. In his family, this appeared very early, by the haughty and imperious conduct of Rehoboam, when advanced to the throne. Nor was it less conspicuous in that of the people. Indolence seems to have formed their character; and to religion they had become insensible. Jeroboam's

* Scap. Lexicon on the word "Onos." † I. Kings, 11. 8.

A2

sagacity perceived this, and his policy took advantage of it. After having built altars, prepared images, and purchased priests, he assembled the people and said: " It is too much for you to go up to Jerusalem : behold thy gods, O Israel, which brought thee up out of the land of Egypt."* How ignorant must they have been of the history of their fathers, and, particularly, of the *calf* of *Aaron* the *priest*,† who could swallow such an absurdity? Yet so ignorant they were. The word of king Jeroboam, and of Jeroboam's pensioned priests, *though of the meanest of the people*, was more to them than the word of God. In obedience to his majesty, they bowed down, with their new-created holy fathers, and reverently worshipped the " calves and the devils,"‡ established as their gods by *royal edict.* With such gods, and under the tuition of such priests, what could be expected among the people, but ignorance, superstition, and immorality, in all their varieties of folly, meanness, deformity and horror! I have mentioned Aaron's calf, and it should never be forgotten. How astonishing does it appear, that the man and family first consecrated to preside in the worship of the only true God, should be the first to pervert, nay, to destroy that worship—to mislead the understanding, and corrupt the hearts of the people, whom they were to instruct in religious truths, and guide in its paths!

In passing through the brief records of the succeeding reigns, down to the Babylonish captivity—a series of 387 years—little occurs but simple facts. The idolatry and other crimes of the people are occasionally mentioned, but no immediate cause is assigned. It is true, national characters generally take their complexion from those of courts. If this be admitted, it will follow, that, in Judah, it must have been generally dark ; and in Israel, gradually proceeding from black to blacker, till every ray of divine light was totally absorbed. In it, the gods of all the different nations, by which it was conquered, or with which it was connected, were successively enrolled with the calves and the devils of Jeroboam, till the people, literally speaking, " knew not what they worshipped."§ From the characters of these objects of worship, the rites performed to their honor, and the indul-

* I. Kings, 12. 28. † Exod. 22. 32. ‡ 2d Chron. 11. 15.
§ John 4. 22.

gences which accompanied them, the hearts of the worshippers must have become, as it were, encrusted with impurity, and their consciences steeled against virtuous sentiment.

Though this conclusion seems just and natural, it conduces nothing to the solution of my enquiries. From a religion, impure in it's source, nothing but streams of impurity can flow. By a religion, whose objects of worship are stained with every vice, nothing can be infused into the minds of the worshippers, by which vice can be checked, or virtue promoted. Under such a religion, to imitate the gods is to act like devils. And, perhaps, from this very circumstance, the " gods, whom blinded nations fear," are called by that name. Still, however, the question recurs, in all its force : " Whence comes it, that the professors of a religion, whose doctrines are pure, whose precepts are strictly moral, whose sanctions are awfully solemn, and infinitely important, and the object of whose worship is absolutely perfect, the Creator and governor of the universe, and final judge of its rational inhabitants, live, as if there was no God, or *their God a Devil?*"

Though, from the nature of national records, and the complexion of their authors, the philosopher, moralist, and divine, seldom derive much instruction, the same cannot be said of the writings of the prophets. The instruction and reformation of the people, are the objects, for the restoration or preservation of which they received their inspiration and commission. And, it is painful to observe, that the necessity of their mission arose from the carelessness, infidelity, and gross corruption of the priests, the *endowed* teachers, and *established* guardians of religion and morals. Had they done their duty, the enormities and profligacy of the magistracy would have been checked, and the virtue of the people preserved.

The pictures which the prophets draw, of the wickedness of the people, are gloomy—of their wretchedness, pitiable. But they resolve both into the tyranny, rapacity, and profligacy of their rulers ; and the sottishness, debauchery, and avarice of their priests. Their language is ; " O my people, they who lead thee cause thee to err, and destroy the way of thy paths !" " Thy princes are roaring lions ; thy judges are ravening wolves." "Thy watchmen are dumb dogs—they are *greedy dogs, which can never have enough*—they all look to their own way, every one for his gain. They riot in wine, and fill themselves with strong drink. They walk in lies; they strengthen also the hands of evil doers so that none doth return from his wickedness. They *bite*, and they cry *peace!* and against him who putteth not into their mouths, they proclaim war. They have devoured SOULS. The priests have profaned my holy things; and, from them, profaneness hath gone forth into all the land. The shepherds slay the flocks, and hold themselves not guilty. They eat the fat, and clothe themselves with the fleece: and they who sell them, say, "*Blessed be the Lord! I am rich.* With force, and with cruelty, have they ruled them. Nay, even the prophets prophesy falsely, and the priests bear rule by their means."

How disgusting must have been the picture, of which the preceding exhibits but a few slight touches! How shocking—how deleterious to the souls of men—the infernal original from which it was taken! Merciful God! What mind, unhackneyed in the ways of corruption, could ever suppose, that thy priests, consecrated to thy service, fed by thine altars, and whose ministry had the promotion of knowledge, truth, righteousness, and holiness among mankind, as it's only immediate object, should deserve to stand in the foreground, amidst such an execrable group! Yet such was the fact. Who, then, can be surprised, that the minds of the people were broken, corrupted, and stupified, as to a sense of every thing dignified, virtuous, or respectable! Tyranny in rulers is sufficient to degrade the spirit; but, in alliance with the tyranny, rapacity, licentiousness, and impiety of the priesthood, it must not only degrade, but pervert, corrupt, and enslave the whole soul. All sense of good and evil, of honor and shame, must be extinguished. Truth itself will lose its relish, and religion become an object of contempt, ridicule, and blasphemy. Or should any faint trace of it remain upon the heart, it will degenerate into superstition, amuse itself with fooleries, and delight in fables, as the only spiritual food which it is capable of digesting.

This was really the case with the Jewish people. Their spirit was so completely broken, that a murmur was not to be heard, though " children were their oppressors, and women ruled over them :" Whilst religion was so far lost, and their taste depraved, that the " prophets not only prophesied falsely, and the priests bare rule by their means," without complaint ; but " the people loved to have it so !"

Alas ! unhappy and deluded people ! Hard was thy lot ! The temple, the scene of thy religious services, was polluted by the licentiousness and impiety of thy priests : the synagogue, the only fountain of thy knowledge, was not only muddied, but poisoned, by the ignorance of thy scribes, and the venality of thy prophets : and, from the throne, except in a few instances, thou hadst nothing to expect. Asa, Jehoshaphat, Hezekiah. and Josiah, formed only a minority in the roll of thy kings. In thy priests and thy rulers, I perceive the source of thy vices, thy meanness, and thy wretchedness. So far, my *curiosity* is satisfied ; but my heart is sick. Pity and indignation share my soul between them.

Surely, however, the scene will brighten, and my sorrows subside, when I look forward to the œconomy of the perfect dispensation of divine knowledge, wisdom, and grace. The circumstances under which it was introduced ; the light which it displayed ; the astonishing facts which proved it's divine original ; the purity and importance of it's precepts ; the prospects of futurity which it unfolded ; the eternal sanctions by which it is enforced ; and the awful responsibility which it denounces, must recommend it to the understanding, and overawe the hearts of all its professors, who receive it in it's genuine simplicity ; whilst the humble, meek, patient, pious, benevolent, forgiving, and, in every particular, sinless example of its author, must stand as an impregnable barrier against anger, impiety, avarice, ambition, cruelty, revenge, and lust, in all it's branches, in succeeding teachers of christian doctrine, and ministers in christian worship.

This seems to be verified in the disciples, during their master's life, with very few exceptions. On one occasion, they shewed an unwarrantable resentment against a Samaritan village ; but their master's reproof seems to have repressed the like ever after. On another, two of them seem to have cherished their ambition and jealousy to a great heighth. However, this was while their understandings were uninformed, and, like their countrymen in general, they expected their master's "kingdom to be of this world," and believed it's honors and emoluments to be fair game for his friends and favorites. From the moment their master set them right on this subject, a symptom of their former passions never appeared. As to Judas, he is said to have been a thief; but whether covetousness was the only passion, which induced him to *make sale* of his master, has been doubted. Be that as it may, he was the first *merchant preacher*, who estimated Christ by what he could make of him, and having closed his sale with the rulers in church and state, pocketed the *Bounty*, and *affectionately* handed *him* over to *their* hireling ruffians. But, be his prevailing passion what it may, it's reign was short. The justice which he did himself and the world, by stepping aside and hanging himself, testified some remains of a virtuous shame, and some symptoms of a sleeping conscience awakened to remorse.

The disciples, raised to the dignity of apostles, after the ascension of their master; those, whom they assumed as assistants in office; and the great body of their early converts; present an uniform appearance of fervent piety, heart-felt generosity, and unbending firmness in the cause of truth, humanity, and religion. The solitary exception of Ananias and Sapphira, and the absurd presumption of Simon Magus, do not deserve to be mentioned, as exceptions to general character. They appear, only as two solitary grains of dust, on the surface of the polished mirror, or two small specks on the disk of the sun.

What a delightful picture this, for the contemplation of the religious eye! But, alas! some scattered hints, and many prophecies, both of Christ and his apostles, excite the painful apprehension, that it is soon to be darkened, disfigured, or even destroyed. Christ warned his followers to " beware of false prophets who would come in sheep's clothing; but inwardly were ravening wolves." Nay, that the impostors would have the presumption to arrogate the characters, " not only of prophets, but of Christs, and would do wonders, was, if possible, to deceive the very elect." And that "through the prevalence of iniquity, the love of many would wax cold." The apostles not only repeat these predictions; but inform us, that, even in their time, there were some of them among the people. Nay, John who lived longest, and wrote latest, of all the apostles, tells us, that "many such were gone out into the world."

Concerning these wretches, our Saviour only informs us, *that they may be known by their characters.* However, the apostles go farther. They delineate their characters plainly, that by their fruits we may know them," and avoid exposing ourselves to contempt, ridicule, or loss, by attempting to "gather grapes of thorns, or figs of thistles." The character, as drawn by them, is the blackest, vilest, and most detestable that ever was delineated by pen of mortal. Would to God! the original had never existed; or that the picture could be obliterated, or concealed for ever! Father of mercy!— Fountain of wisdom!—forgive the presumption of a weak—but well meaning—mortal! If thou, by the voice of prophets, or the pen of inspiration, hast exposed the ungainly monsters, in all their deformity, that thy simple, unsuspecting children may be on their guard against the hypocrisy, falshood, covetousness, and ambition, and their accursed example—*the poison of souls!* —more destructive than all! what am I that I should arraign thy wisdom, or wish the expressions of thy mercy concealed! Father, forgive me! I see my error, and disclaim it. Though I shudder, and shrink from the picture before me; yet, as the pencil of inspired knowledge hath drawn it, and the pencil of inspiration cannot falsify—I will copy it with faithfulness—I will hold it up to the world—While I live, I will lift up my voice—I will proclaim in the ears of all the people, " *Ye children of the highest, behold and tremble: Beware! Beware! ye redeemed of the Lord!"* The monsters have propagated their kind, and encreased in their number. As they have multiplied, their malignity has gained strength—temporary success has added to their insolence—and the savory taste, which they have had, of the price of souls, has whetted their appetite for a full meal. Again, I say, " Beware! Beware! It is not only the rapacity of the and counteract, but the cunning of the fox, the poison of the serpent, and the impudence of the devil.

"Seducing spirits, speaking lies in hypocrisy; by flattering words and fair speeches, deceiving the hearts of the simple, and leading them into offence and divisions merely to serve their own bellies.—Deceitful workers, transforming themselves into apostles of Christ, as Satan transforms himself into an angel of light—creeping into houses, and leading captive silly women laden with sin—proud, covetous, boasters, blasphemers, false accusers, despisers of honest men, headstrong, lovers of pleasure, more than lovers of God, having a form of religion, but belying it's power, having their consciences seared with an hot iron—ever learning, and never coming to the knowledge of the truth, unruly and vain talkers, teachers of what they ought not for filthy lucre's sake, turning aside to vain jangling, giving themselves up to old wives' fables, *eternal genealogies*, and silly questions, which serve only to promote discord, envy, and contention.—Through covetousnes making merchandize of the flock of Christ, sensual, presumptuous, speaking evil of things which they understand not, beguiling unstable souls, and sporting themselves with their own deceptions—wells without water; tempestuous clouds, thundering out great swelling words of vanity; turning the grace of God into lasciviousness, and going after strange flesh—filthy dreamers! cursed children! who have forsaken the path of rectitude, and followed the way of Balaam, for the wages of unrighteousness."

This picture is not more full of horror, than the fate which awaits the originals, is full of awe. "Their *judgment* lingereth not—their *damnation* doth not slumber."

When we view the preceding picture, and reflect on the declaration annexed, we must see that the benevolent John must have had pleasure in declaring, that, though the BLACK originals went out from the little synod of the apostles, "they were not of them;" and that it was "manifest" to the world, "they were not." Would to God, that all succeeding ministers of the word of truth and righteousness, could, *with truth*, declare the same of all such ministers! We must perceive also, that, wherever such appear, in the character of ministers of religion, the people must be more stupified and insensible, than the ass of Balaam, who do not raise their voice to rebuke their madness, meanness, and profligacy.

Soon, after I had proceeded thus far, the volumes, promised by my friend, reached me—I seized them with avidity, and, under all the gloom diffused over my mind, by the predictions of the divine Author of our religion, and the commencement of their verification, in the days of his apostles, I proceeded to peruse them.

During the first two centuries, little occurred direct to my purpose. Many of the pretended records are evidently spurious. In those, admitted as genuine, piety, zeal, and simplicity, characterise the propagators and first preachers of the gospel; and the people, in general, seem to have been guided and profited by their example. It is true, as these primitive teachers had been differently educated, and accustomed to different forms and times, in the externals of religion, they brought with them prejudices, principles, and practices, which tended to adulterate, disfigure, and weaken the heavenly system, and embroil them in controversies, not only useless, but hurtful. The difference of a day or two, in the celebration of Easter, a festival merely Jewish, and unauthorised by Christ or his apostles, had nearly separated the Asiatic and western churches in the latter end of the second century, and occasioned repeated disputes between those of the Latins and Greeks, till their final separation.

Avarice and ambition seem not to have been felt by the teachers of that period. They appear to have been incessant in their labors, patient in adversity, in poverty content, unshaken by persecution, and, so far from avoiding martyrdom, they frequently courted it. Several of their writings abound with learning, both sacred and profane. Many opinions of the different philosophic sects are interspersed with the christian doctrines. But few of these thorny questions, which afterwards perplexed the world, split christians into parties, and destroyed genuine christianity, were yet started. Hence the laity lived in love and peace among themselves. The character of christians, as a body, may be fairly estimated by Tertullian's account of them. "We make up a body united by the bond of the same religion, and the same hope. We assemble ourselves to pray, not only for ourselves, but for the emperors, the ministers, the magistrates, and the good of the state. Besides, we assemble to read the holy Scriptures, for our instruction, and information in our duty. These sacred oracles preserve our faith, confirm our hope, and regulate our manners. In these assemblies, necessary reproofs and exhortations are to be expected. The judgments, there delivered, are given with all imaginable equity and circumspection. The censures are all divine. Those who preside amongst us, are the most antient, and those whose probity is very well known; and this honor is not to be purchased for money. It is bestowed upon pure virtue; for those concerns which relate to God, are not to be valued at a price. If we have any treasure, every one contributes, according to his ability, what alms he pleases, and when he pleases; yet this is commonly done monthly. None are compelled. Every one gives freely. These contributions are the contributions of piety; for we do not employ them in making merry meetings, or other unnecessary expences; but to maintain and bury orphans, and poor people, to relieve the old and infirm, to *assist the faithful, who are exiled, imprisoned, or condemned to the mines,* for having embraced the faith of Jesus Christ. We all call ourselves brethren, not only because we are so by nature, but because we acknowledge the same God as our father—because we have all the same spirit which makes us holy—and lastly, because all things are common among us, except our women. Our feasts are entertainments of love and charity. They were not instituted for debauched parasites, but for the entertainment of the poor : and, if sacred in their institution, in their consequences they are equally sacred. Nothing is there to be seen contrary to civility and modesty. They are preceded by prayer, for the nourishment of the soul. We eat only to suffice nature, and drink no more than is becoming chaste and moderate persons. We discourse only of things profitable, because we consider ourselves as in the presence of God— the witness of all we say. The supper is concluded with prayer. We retire without tumult or disorder, as is easy for persons to do, who are more anxious to nourish their souls with the holy discipline in which they are instructed, than their bodies with the victuals which they eat."

What a delightful picture this! How happy the symmetry in all its parts! How divine the colouring! Behold the ministers of Jesus as they ought to be, pious, meek, patient, and zealous in their duty; neither enslaved by the corruptions of the world, hunting after its deceitful and accursed riches, nor proudly aspiring to be *lords over God's heritage*; but humbly satisfied with the more becoming honor of being *examples to the flock*; and, behold the sheep of the fold obedient to their voice —walking in their steps—docile, mild, charitable, sober, social, and devout! Surely, were the ministers of religion ever such, the professors of religion would be such also.

In the third age, some shades begin to be cast over the christian system and character. The usurpations of imagination, over the provinces of reason and understanding, shew themselves in the mode of interpreting scripture. These usurpations give rise to questions, not only impertinent, but presumptuous—Questions! to the terms of which no precise meaning has, even yet, been affixed. These questions were discussed with a degree of passion and virulence, exactly, in an inverse ratio of the knowledge and intellect of the disputants. In the contest, temper was lost, and revelation stood aghast. Doctrines were taken for granted and affirmed, which the assertors, themselves, allowed to be not only *uncomprehended*, but *incomprehensible*. This consequence was absolutely unavoidable. In every argument, where premisses are expressed in terms, to which no idea can be affixed, the conclusion must be a happy random-stroke of blind conjecture; or must, infinitely, *rise above*, or *sink below* all possibility of comprehension. To these questions, disputes, and diversity of doctrine arising from them, the famous Origen contributed not a little: and if nothing else can be said of him, it may be asserted that he supplied the matter of many disputes never yet settled, nor ever likely to be so, in this world, unless God, of his infinite goodness, shall give men sense to perceive, and grace to acknowledge, " IN THE REVELATIONS OF HIS WISDOM AND WILL TO MEN, HE HATH SPOKEN TO THEIR UNDERSTANDINGS; AND THAT, BY THE USE OF THAT UNDERSTANDING, THE MEANING OF HIS INSPIRED WORD MAY BE CLEARLY DISCOVERED, AND FULLY ASCERTAINED."

Cyprian, bishop of Carthage, about the middle of this century, gave rise to great feuds between the Italian and African bishops, on a variety of subjects; particularly, about the validity of baptism by heretics. This Cyprian denied: and Stephen, bishop of Rome, asserted it, with much heat, and great virulence; pronouncing all who differed from him, *" false Christians, false apostles, and seducers."* Union seems, from this time to lose its hold on the ministers of religion. Disputing about its forms, they lost its spirit. Forms usurped the attention due to principle and purity. Ceremonies gained a footing in the church latterly. The table of the Lord was transformed into an altar, the commemorative bread and wine into a sacrifice, and the ministers into priests.

About this time, and in the beginning of the fourth century, some very learned men appeared, as Arnobius, Lactantius, and Eusebius of Cæsarea. The two former sensibly exposed the rage of the day, for disputing about *incomprehensibles*; and the Chronicon of the latter is a most valuable book.

However, as in the fourth century, the external state of the church underwent a great revolution; and a new æra may be said to commence; let us pause for a moment, and cast a glance backward on the three preceding.

During them, even the votaries of the multiplied rites, pompous pageantry, and canonized mummery, of succeeding ages, admit, that the discipline was simple, the doctrine apostolical, and the morality pure. " Their discipline," say they, " was plain and simple; without splendor, *except what the holiness of the manners and lives of the Christians* gave it. They assembled every Sunday in particular, and continued long in prayer, which they pronounced in a low voice, without chanting. The bishop, or in his absence, one of the deacons read the scriptures; and the bishop frequently preached the word of God. The places, where they met, were without ornament, and the use of images, crosses, and incense, was not common. (they might have said, " known") They observed the festivals of the nativity, Easter and Whitsunday. On Sundays, and from Easter to Whitsunday, they prayed standing. They had frequent feasts of charity, where all guests were kindly entertained. They commemorated the dead by prayers and oblations. They baptized converts, by immersion. Scandalous offences were punished, in the laity, by exclusion from communion, fasts and mortifications; and in the clergy, by deprivation, for life. He, who was excommunicated in one church, was rejected by all. The matter of the Eucharist was ordinary bread and wine, in some churches, mingled with water. After thanksgiving by the bishop, or presbyter, the bread was broken into small pieces, and the deacons distributed it and the wine among the congregation. They received the Eucharist, generally, at all their meetings for public worship; and considered it as a solemn obligation to a pious and christian life. They were very careful to choose, as ministers, men of unblamable life. After the death of those, who were ordained by the apostles, the *people elected* their *ministers*. Superiority among bishops, in rule and jurisdiction, was unknown. Infallibility was undreamed of. They respected the divisions of councils. The clergy were distinguished, not by their habit, but the purity of their lives. *They exhibited no symptom of the vile lust of gain.* Tithes were unknown. The voluntary contributions of the people formed the only maintenance of their ministers; and the offerings of the pious were reserved for the poor. The clergy were prohibited from all civil and secular offices, and did not remove from one church to another, through avarice and ambition. They were examples of charity and correctness. Marriage was allowed: yet many, both male and female lived in celibacy. They abstained from blood, things strangled or offered to idols."

This was the general state of discipline, though, in some churches, particularly those of Africa, many peculiarities had begun to shew themselves.

Their general doctrine was, simply that of the scriptures; though tradition was sometimes called in. Indeed, they were so near the source, that some confidence might be placed in the purity of the streams. Their principal disputes were about the Godhead. They, generally, rejected the term " Generation," as to the Son, and preferred that of " Prolatation" or " Emission," from which, it would seem, that they considered the " word" mentioned in scripture, not as a " person," but, simply, as a " word," viz. *an expression of the wisdom and the will of God.* Concerning the nature of the soul, they were divided in opinion. Some believed it to be material; some not. But it's immortality, and a future state of retribution, do not appear to have been doubted. They asserted the freedom of the will. They taught the inspiration of the holy scriptures, and their sufficiency as a rule of faith. Their canon was the same as ours; though, sometimes, they quoted the apocryphal books.

Their morality was conformable with their doctrine; and, probably, more perfectly scriptural. They inculcated all the laws of the gospel, as the rule of christian conduct, under the sanctions of christianity; and, what is more, they exemplified them in their lives. The boast of one of the christian apologists, may seem proud, but it was never controverted: " Non eloquimur magna, sed vivimus."—*We speak not great things, but we live them.*

In the fourth age, the christian church assumes a new form; and, I am sorry to say, displays a new spirit. Disputes among the clergy, were carried on with great rancour, and christians split into parties, mutually persecuted each other with violence and cruelty. The conversion of Constantine, while it gave the christians liberty and protection in the public possession and exercise of their religion, did not, eventually, serve its interests. Lands and revenues were granted to the church, the produce of which were, at first, wisely disposed of, one portion being allowed to the bishop, one to the inferior ministers of religion, one to the poor, and the fourth to the erection and support of places of worship. The bishops, however, now a superior order, and vested with authority as judges of the land, being the managers, soon began to enrich themselves, and, through the influence of riches, to aim at power and pre-eminence in the state. The division of the empire into ecclesiastical provinces and districts, and modelling the rank, jurisdiction, and authority of the clergy, on the plan of the civil government, was highly favorable to the views of covetousness and ambition. The clergy soon became rich and powerful: and, possessed of riches and power, they became licentious, proud, and tyrannical. To be convinced of this, nothing more is necessary than a glance at the records of the numerous councils, in this century. In almost every page canons present themselves, not only respecting their licentiousness, avarice, and ambition, but even violations of nature. The people, too, overawed by their power, and corrupted by their example, degenerated with them.

The public doctrine of this age was nearly the same with that of the preceding, except what was introduced, by the council of Nice, about the Trinity, in consequence of the Arian controversy. And of that council it is remarkable, that, though they decreed peremptorily, and anathematized boldly, they acknowledged the subject of their decree, and the foundation of their anathema, " *incomprehensible and ineffable.*" Indeed, concerning their principal word—the Greek word, " Hypostasis"—they were not agreed, in any manner. One party maintained that it signifies " *Nature* or *Substance*," as the Greek church still does: another, that it means " PERSON," which is, and uniformly has been, the doctrine of the church of Rome. Again, some asserted, be the meaning what it may, the Father, Son, and holy Spirit were three *Hypostases ;* and others, that they were but one.

In discipline and modes of worship, an astonishing change now appears. The holy simplicity of the three former ages is no longer to be observed, either in the government, policy, or worship of the church. Subordination is introduced in churches, and consequently, in their bishops. Civil provinces form the body, and mark the bounds, of ecclesiastical. The bishop of the civil metropolis is dubbed first bishop of the province, with rights, prerogatives, and revenues annexed. And, as many civil provinces formed a district, called " Diocess," as many ecclesiastical did the same, and the bishop of the principal city had rights, prerogatives, and privileges of honor and jurisdiction, over the whole diocess, together with the power of ordaining his metropolitans, which formerly belonged to the bishops of the province. The metropolitan presided in provincial ordinations ; but, still, the people had a share in the elections. Rome, as yet, neither possessed nor claimed supremacy. When her bishops abused their power, they were subject, as individuals, to the correction of their brother bishops, as a body. Alexandria, Antioch, Jerusalem, and Constantinople, had, by ecclesiastical custom, some particular privileges, in common with Rome. Metropolitans ruled the churches of Spain and Gaul. In Africa, this dignity belonged to the oldest bishop of the province; though the bishop of Carthage had some peculiar rights and prerogatives. Beyond the limits of the Roman empire, forms were unsettled: but each church had its own bishop.

In ecclesiastical matters, the clergy sat in judgment with the bishop. Differences among bishops were settled by provincial councils, which, commonly, met twice a year. Matters of faith were reserved for general councils. Excommunication was the ecclesiastical penalty, for all errors and crimes. The churches were united by letters of communion. In the west, celibacy began to be enjoined on the higher orders. The sacraments were administered *gratis*. Such good canons as were made, were rendered futile, by the *ambition* and *covetousness* of the bishops, the arbitrary will of princes, and the interested passions of men. In the services of religion, pomp and splendor superseded simplicity and plainness. Baptism was administered by triple dipping, and many other ceremonies. Exorcisms and anointings were used; and milk and honey given to the catechumens. The eucharist was given in both kinds. The Agapæ, or love-feasts began to be abolished. The scriptures were publicly read, and sermons delivered. Singing psalms was in use. The dead were commemorated at the celebration of the eucharist. Festivals to saints and martyrs were instituted. Crosses, and the sign of the cross, were used. In some churches, images were introduced. Most churches had deaconesses; but the number of the lower orders of the clergy was unfixed. Fasting, at particular seasons, and on set days, was strictly observed. The monastic state took a settled form. Both monks and nuns were subject to bishops. There were a few hermits; and some undertook pilgrimages; but, such journies were not much approved.

From the middle of this century, the clergy, while they despised and tyrannized over the people, were the mean sycophants of the civil power; and, so early as the year 359, four hundred western bishops, of the council of Ariminum, rescinded all their decrees, by the mandate of the emperor, and subscribed the creed sent them,

At Selencia, 160 did the same. The words of the historian are, " *The emperor approved, and all parties subscribed the Nicene Creed.*"

The frivolity of the ceremonies, about the end of this century, may be judged of, by the two following examples: The Arians, and six other sects of those called " Heretics," having anathematized their errors, and professed the *orthodox* faith, were received into communion, " *by the unction of the Holy Spirit, and the application of chrism to their foreheads, eyes, hands, mouths and ears, at the pronouncing of these words:* THIS IS THE SEAL OF THE HOLY SPIRIT." The Eunomians, and all other heretics were considered in a worse light. They were received by " the imposition of hands, exorcisms, blowing *three times* into their faces and ears; and," after a long probation, " by baptism."

How must the clergy have been lost to all decency, common sense, and regard to the word of God, when they adopted, and imposed such mummeries! How must the people have been debased, corrupted, and blinded by superstition, before they submitted to such fooleries! With such a priesthood, what virtue—what sense of God, the only foundation on which virtue can stand secure—could be expected among the people! Alas! *none.*

From what has been observed, of the doctrine and discipline of the age, it would be vain to look for an improvement in, or even the preservation of, *pulpit* morality.

The next century commences with an increase of clerical adulation to men in power, clerical riches, and clerical wrangling. The subjects of controversy became more numerous, the terms used, more unmeaning, and the spirit, with which they were agitated, more envenomed and rancorous. The arm of civil power was called in to execute the sentence of ecclesiastical phrenzy. The most prominent object, before the middle of the century, was the phrase, " MOTHER OF GOD," then first introduced. Nestorius, bishop of Constantinople, rejected it. This occasioned a ferment so great, that the emperor, Theodosius the younger, in the year 431, called a council at Ephesus, to allay it, the history of which may serve as a specimen of the learning, religion and temper of the age. Mutual excommunications, persecutions, and a total submission of christian faith and discipline to imperial mandates, mark their sittings: while their ravings about " MOTHER, AND NO MOTHER OF GOD."— " ONE SON, AND TWO SONS—" GENERATION, IN TIME, AND BEFORE TIME"—" ONE NATURE, AND TWO NATURES"—" THE IMMORTAL IS DEAD"—" GOD IS CRUCIFIED"—" MIXTURE, AND NO MIXTURE," &c. &c. —have served, and still serve, only to give edge to the weapons of the infidel against our faith; to inspire the wise man with contempt; and overwhelm the pious christian with a mixture of pity, sorrow, and indignation.

During the succeeding part of this century, little else occurs, but repetitions of such vain janglings, and the feuds, excommunications, persecutions, &c. of which they were productive. Some of the councils enacted wise canons respecting the conduct of the clergy; yet these very canons prove the prevailing irregularity of their lives; and probably owe their existence to the influence of the emperors, princes, and lords, who sat with the bishops and clergy.

Next to theological wrangling, the increase and distribution of church-revenues, now become great, engaged their attention, and were the subject of their decrees. On the whole, the complexion of this age, bears some resemblance to that of the former; but its shades are rather darker. In doctrine, Scripture was less attended to. The *Faith of the church* was erected into an *infallible standard.* Hence, absurdity gained ground; the doctrines of men were substituted for the counsels of God; ceremonies increased in number, and pomp; superstition spread her gloomy reign; new orders were introduced into the clergy; monks began to aspire to power; and morality drooped.

In the beginning of the sixth century, the canons of some councils entirely respect the security and enlargement of church revenues; of others, the villainies of the clergy; which, it would seem, no punishments could completely prevent, or restrain. Covetousness, now predominant, led to the meanest flattery of the rich and great, in order to preferment; and to jealousies, calumnies, false accusations, and every vile mean of supplanting a rival, and rising upon his ruin to favour and riches.

.Hence the strict laws of, almost, every council, against these degrading vices, and the severity of the penalties, with which they were enacted.

From the year 457 to 536, the city of Alexandria exhibited a continued scene of the persecutions, excommunications, and barbarities, of succeeding patriarchs and their partizans. Power and emolument seem to have been their only objects. Whether the " *body of Christ was corruptible, or incorruptible,*" was a prime subject of debate. In it, successive emperors took an active part, and on different sides. Justinian, and his empress Theodora took the field against each other; and their respective favorites were deposed, anathematized, and banished, in turn. The council of Constantinople, in 536, issued several condemnations, in all which Justinian interposed his authority by public edicts. Some of the charges, on which these were founded, were ridiculous; others, highly disgraceful to the clergy of the day. That against Peter of Apamæi, may serve as an example of both. He addressed himself, thus, to some of his readers, who desired to be promoted to holy orders: " Unless ye hold your peace, I will ordain you all sub-deacons; and, when the crucified man shall descend, he shall not pluck you out of my hand."

About the year 541, confusion still prevailing, in Egypt and the East, Justinian eagerly seized an opportunity of making a figure on the ecclesiastical stage; and, in conjunction with Pelagius, surrogate of Rome, and some Egyptian monks, issued a long anathematizing edict, against Origen, and a train of his errors. The first of these was about the Trinity; the second, the Plurality of worlds; third, the Pre-existence of Souls; fourth, That the Heavens and Stars are animated; fifth, That the glorified Bodies shall be of a round figure; and sixth, That the torments of the damned shall have an end.

Anathemas against these *heresies*, with others against many individuals, the wise, enlightened, and pious council of Constantinople, broken to the purpose in the imperial Menagerie, solemnly confirmed.

Vigilius, bishop of Rome, was enraged at these proceedings, and separated from the communion of the *confirming* bishops. However, softened by the empress, he soon after, by a decree, confirmed their judgment. By this, the bishops of Africa, Illyria, and Dalmatia, were enraged, in their turn; and those of Gaul and Italy caught the flame. The Pope, perplexed, revoked his decree; which called forth the rage of the emperor, who, in his turn, published a new edict, in the year 551. The Pope anathematized all who should receive it, and fled from imperial vengeance. After various displays of fortitude and meanness; after seven years of prevarication, artifice, and packing of councils; and after being banished, for opposing the sentence of councils; *his Holiness* meanly recanted, made the most humiliating submissions, retracted all his writings, on the subjects in dispute, and anathematized those who should defend them. The emperor relented, recalled, and restored him. But he died, in his return to Italy, in the year 558, leaving behind him the character of meanness and villainy, without having reaped their fruits, or enjoyed them, even for a day.

After the death of Vigilius, Justinian rigorously persecuted all the bishops who had opposed him; and the conduct of the clergy, towards each other, was horrid and execrable. Though all agreed in the general creeds; though all acknowledged the authority of the same councils; yet all, in turn, accused, condemned, persecuted, and excommunicated one another. And it is remarkable that, in all their debates and decisions, during a succession of councils, for twenty two years, there is not a single allusion to Scripture, or any thing contained in it, except one to the meeting of the first christians, in Jerusalem, about the terms of receiving the Gentile converts; and this was with a view to establish their own sovereign authority, as a council.

The remaining forty years of this century present some variety, in the records of its numerous councils. In that variety, however, there is scarcely so much good, as to make the bad tolerable. The frequency of canons against incontinence, in the clergy; the strict prohibitions against having women in their houses; the restraints upon female visits, even to bishops, with the number and *sanctity* of the witnesses to be present; and many other circumstances, fix a dark stain on the clerical character. Next to these, the most prominent object is church-revenue. The security and increase of it forms the matter of a great majority of the canons, in every council. Tithes are brought into view; their divine original asserted; their long disuse mentioned with regret; and their revival warmly recommended to the *pious* and *faithful.* However, the ends to which they were to be applied, are highly praiseworthy—" THE RELIEF OF THE POOR, AND REDEMPTION OF CAPTIVES." The interference of emperors and princes, in ecclesiastical affairs, gave rise to some canons favorable to the rights of the laity. That of electing bishops was declared to be in the people and clergy: the prince was not to nominate, nor the elected to be ordained, without the approbation of the metropolitan. The clergy, however, begin to lift their heads. They declare it unlawful for any judge to take cognizance of the causes of bishops. They forbid priests, deacons, &c. to be accused before any judges. They demand as a right, from the laity, even the salutations of civility, and in a humiliating manner. On the whole, the clerical character becomes more ungainly; the interference of the state, in the concerns of religion, becomes more bold; form and frippery continue to infringe upon principle, and the people to sink deeper in ignorance, superstition, and depravity. What else could be expected, when, not only ignorance and avarice; fornication and adultery; but theft, robbery, murder, and sacrilege, marked the characters of their spiritual guides; and the lands of the clergy were cultivated by slaves, attached to the soil!

It should not pass unnoticed, that the residence of the emperors, in Constantinople, gave great authority to that See; that the council of Chaludon gave it all the rights, privileges, and prerogatives, claimed or exercised by that of Rome; that its bishop, afterwards, elated by ambition, assumed the title of " UNIVERSAL PATRIARCH;" and that Gregory 1st, of Rome, so far from arrogating supremacy, pronounced such a title " *proud, heretical, blasphemous, antichristian, and diabolical,*" and exerted all his learning and rhetoric, both with the emperor Maurice, and the eastern bishops, to prove his assertion. He condemned the worship of images. In his answer to a letter of Eulogius, patriarch of Alexandria, highly flattering to the see of Rome ; there is a passage truly curious: " Though there were many apostles," says he, " yet there was but one see of the prince of the apostles. This see is in three places ; at Rome, where he finished his course ; at Alexandria, whither he sent his evangelist, St. Mark, to supply the place ; and at Antioch, where he continued seven years. But *these three sees are but one see,* which belongs to St. Peter ; in which *three bishops* now sit, *who are in effect but one,* in him who prayed : that they may be one, as I am in the father, and the father in me."

Is this jest, or earnest ? Be which it may, surely it is a bitter sarcasm against the doctrine of the trinity ; or, at least, an explicit declaration that the unity in trinity is *merely moral.*

He supported a good character, having done much, and attempted more, to reform the clergy. His soliciting the civil power to harrass the Jews leaves a reproach on his name, or rather, on the times. He sat in the chair of Rome, near fourteen years ; assuming, in his pastoral letters, the modest title ; " *servant of the servants of God,"* and died in 604.

In the seventh and eighth centuries, the character of the clergy, and the state of the christian world, take a darker hue, than in any of the former. The remains of learning, judgment, taste, and eloquence, can scarcely be traced ; though attempts began to be made to methodize science, and reduce religious doctrines to system. Such useful canons as were framed by councils to restrain the irregularity of clergy, or people, were so little respected, that the civil power was obliged to interpose in their execution. The councils of Spain, France, and England, should rather be considered as parliaments, as princes, nobles, &c. sat in them ; and their canons respected the government of the state, as much as that of the church. In the pulpit, fable usurped the place of truth and knowledge. The pen was equally misapplied. New penitentials, instead of improving, corrupted, discipline ; and casuistry, which ought to have secured, destroyed morality. Auricular confession became common. The donations of the kings of France clothed the popes with riches, honors, and temporal sovereignty. Notwithstanding the exertions of princes, ignorance and licentiousness reigned among the bishops and clergy. Some good men, among the former, in order to restrain the enormities of the inferior orders, were obliged to shut them up in cloysters, which gave rise to the order of *canons regular*. The adoration of images was now introduced, and superstition triumphed. Still, however, the eucharist was administered in both kinds.

A few extracts from the canons of councils, and historical records, in these two ages, will confirm what I have written.

Gregory first gave a sanction to lighted tapers in the church, in open day; Leo 3d, in 794, commanded the priests to burn incense at the altars of the saints; and holy water began to be used. Both practices were copied from the pagan liturgy. About the year 750, Pope Zachary enjoined some German monks, *not to eat their bacon, till after easter, unless dried in the smoke, or dressed at the fire.*

In the year 6c1, Ethelbert, king of England, at the instigation of Augustine, made war upon his people, and put to the sword 1200 monks of the monastery of Bangor, because they would not conform to the customs of the Roman church, respecting easter, baptism, &c.

The council of Lateran, in 649, was entirely taken up with the question; "whether there be, in Christ, one Will and one Operation; or two Wills and two Operations?" about which the Latin and Greek churches differed. After much debate, and the introduction of some new terms, such as "Theandric," "Deivirile," &c. they came to the following wise conclusion: "A man may say, that there was in Christ, ONE WILL, AND TWO WILLS."

Such trimming, and such absurdity, as might be expected, failed of uniting the two churches. The emperor, Constantinus Pogonatus, was therefore obliged to call the third council of Constantinople, which, after sitting, nearly a year, decreed the *orthodoxy* of the *two-will doctrine*; but nothing else.

The councils of Toledo, between the years 650, and 660, present a new scene. The clergy of Spain had, in the *fury of loyalty*, taken a solemn oath "*that they would put to death all, who should be found concerned in any conspiracy against the prince or state.*"

On this, king Receswinthe addressed a letter to the *loyal fathers*, of the eighth council of Toledo, exhorting them " to provide against the disorders they would create, if they attempted to execute their pious oath." Blush! Blush! ye clerical prostitutes. The good king covers you with shame.

The reverend fathers were neither dull of hearing, slow of faith, nor unwilling to obey. They immediately published a long dissertation on the nature of oaths, adduced numberless authorities of scripture, and *the fathers*, to prop it's every part, to convince the world, that men ought not to keep, or execute, oaths, by which they have sworn to commit actions prejudicial to the state.

Who can blame such declaration? But whence proceeded the conviction which gave it birth? Where were the scriptures, the decrees of the fathers, the light of the understanding, and the remonstrances of conscience on this subject, before the receipt of his majesty's letter? Where were they? They were in the pocket of priestly policy, waiting for the accident of a moment, the nod of a minister, or the mandate of a prince. Had the good Receswinthe approved their oath, and enjoined its execution, they would have attempted to justify it, at the expense both of *scripture and fathers.*—Nay, they would have executed it, if assassination, or the hiring of assassins could have sufficed. But, I am convinced, they would not have risqued the effusion of *clerical* blood. Meanness, avarice, and superstition, are all akin to cruelty; and all the family are *cowards*. They will bluster, boast, and calumniate, at a distance; assassinate, either life or character, in the dark; and look bold, behind the shield, or spear of power: but no one of them has ever yet been known, fairly, and on equal ground, to look principle, integrity, or courage, straight in the face.

The *moderation* of the bishops, after the royal monition, appears in their tenth canon, in which they prescribe the mode of electing kings, and enumerate their qualifications. And, in the tenth council of Toledo, in the year 656, they preserve the same character. They confine their sentence against sedicious priests and monks, to deprivation of dignity; leaving the power of restoration to the king. And in the sixteenth council of the same place, in 693, they appear more loyal, but less moderate. They decreed deposition, excommunication for life, confiscation of goods, and perpetual imprisonment against all conspirators : and their tenth canon pronounces Anathema, *three times*, against all who attempt the life of kings, or plot against them or the state ; and *condemns them and their posterity to the condition of slaves.*

It should have been observed as a prelude to these canons, that the sixth council of Toledo, in the year 638, piously thanked king Cinthilu for the expulsion of the Jews ; ordered that succeeding kings should be bound *by oath,* " *not to tolerate infidels ;*" pronounced an anathema against all, who should break such oath ; and enacted that none but a *noble Goth,* should be advanced to the sovereignty.

It should also be observed, that all these councils were more properly parliaments, the nobles having sitten with the clergy ; and that, in each council, there are, at least, two canons in favor of the riches and power of the church, for one, in favor of the crown, or of the state.

The assemblies in England and France, in the eighth century, as in the former, were also of a mixed nature ; embraced both civil and ecclesiastical government, and may, therefore, be considered as parliaments, rather than councils, in the common acceptation of these terms.

Wherever loyalty and church revenues are out of sight, nothing appears but canons against the incontinence and other vices of the clergy, the exclusion of women from monasteries, the necessary restraint of *vagabond monks,* and the excesses of bishops.

It is not unworthy of notice, that, in Britain, the public services of religion, were performed in the Latin tongue, at this time. This, however, is no support to the continuance of that custom. The Romans promoted, as far as possible, the use of their language in the provinces. And, from the long residence of the Roman legions in Britain, the Latin can hardly be supposed to have become an " unknown tongue."

The contest concerning images, began about the year 725. Leo, emperor of the east, warmly opposed their use, as objects of worship. Gregory 2d, and some other bishops were as warm in their favor. The debate between the emperor and pope continued many years.—In it, the pope declared that St. Peter was to be considered as " *a* GOD *upon earth* ;" and that he (Gregory) and the bishop of Constantinople, had the power of " *binding and loosing in heaven,* and on *earth.*" All this did not prevent Leo from issuing an edict, in 730, ordering images to be removed from places of worship, and burned ; and enacting penalties against such as disobeyed it.

Constantine Copronymus, Leo's son, being of the same mind, called a council at Constantinople, in 754, which consisted of nearly 350 bishops, and in which the use and worship of images was condemned. Their decree was rejected by the Romans ; but most of the eastern churches received and executed it.

Thus the matter stood, till the death of Leo the 4th, who succeeded his brother Constantine, in the empire. On this event, Irene, his widow, a woman notorious for cruelty, an attachment to sorcery, and a zealot for images, became mistress of the empire, during the minority of her son Constantine. Under her sway, a new scene presents itself. A council of bishops assembled at Constantinople, in 786, was dissolved. After this, the empress, in her own name and that of her son, assembled a council at Nice, in 787, where the pope's legates, several patriarchs, and archbishops, with 250 bishops, and 100 presbyters, attended. Those who were known to be against image-worship were excluded the council, by the empress' guards. The opposite party established idolatry by canon, and the empress engaged to enforce their constitutions.

The detail of the conduct of bishops, in this council, would be equally uninteresting to the well-informed, and painful to the good. Suffice it to observe, that the bishops, who had zealously and successfully put down idolatry in the councils of Constantinople, were the most forward to restore her altars, and embellish her temples, at Nice. They crouded one after another, with solemn recantations of their former errors, long-winded creeds, belching out the *orthodoxy* of the empress, and copious declarations that they honored, reverenced, and worshipped the images of Christ, the Virgin, the holy Angels, and all the Saints : on which they were restored to favor,

After this, all went on smooth and easy. Idolatry was canonized. Holy and venerable images were licensed for exposure, " in churches, upon sacred vessels, sacerdotal vestments, walls, and tables, in houses, and in the highways." A letter is written and carried by the patriarch, &c. to Constantinople, to give an account of the proceedings of the council, to the emperor and empress. Being arrived there, they are *graciously received*, and kindly entertained. The *pious* Irene, aware of the incense to be offered her, *condescended* to express her wish to be present at the public reading of the canons and decrees of the reverend synod. She was indulged. Dupin's relation of the scene is worth attention, but is too long for transcription.—She attended ; caused the decrees of the council to be read, and, asked, whether they had been unanimously enacted. She was answered by acclamations ; on which she received the record, from the hands of the patriarch, subscribed it, and caused her *dutiful* son to do the same. Acclamations succeeded acclamations of " long life to the EMPRESS ! *Long life to the emperor !*" (the emperor was not yet in power.) The authorities on which the decrees were founded, were then read to the *lords and the people*. Repeated acclamations followed, in which the holy bishops took the lead, the temporal lords followed, and the silly people, the dupes of both, brought up the rear ! What a scene must this have appeared to an enlightened and religious mind, had such been present ! How must such a mind have felt, on hearing the ministers of religion lift up their voice to flatter an abandoned woman, and seeing them pay to her a worship as unmerited, profane, and impious, as they had shamelessly decreed to painted paper, parchment, or canvas—to molten metal, or carved wood ! Let such a mind reflect, for a moment, and feelings will subside. Irene possessed the power and the *purse* of the state— she was the head of the church—preferment and riches were in her hand—*poor clergy* must live—*rich* and *great clergy* would be *richer* and *greater.* In such a case, what is religion but a name—principle, a creature of imagination—and honor, a gaudy shadow ! There is something more fascinating to a *base* mind, in the idea of " *higher class,* a richer living, and the smile of *him,* or *her,* on whom these depend, than in the prospects of heaven, or of the favor of heaven's king." Less than half a century, (the times of Leo and Irene) affords proof sufficient of the fact. Let Leos reign, and the clergy will sacrifice every thing (their benefices are out of the question, and their lives are of no consequence) rather than corrupt the worship of God. Give the sceptre to Irene, and they will bow before the images of Christ, the Virgin, Angels, Saints—ay! of the Devil himself—at her nod. Nay, religion, honor, and the souls of men, will be sacrificed, in a moment, to benefice, dignity, or *classification of bounty.*

In France, pictures were admitted in churches, but every idea of worshipping them was rejected with horror. Charles, the great, had a treatise composed and published against the arguments, authorities, and decrees of this council. It was divided into four parts, which were called the Caroline Books. Amidst the fooleries of the age, they exhibit much good sense, and some learning. The pope answered these books, but to little effect. In the end, image-worship prevailed in the east, and the Italians adopted it. The French, Germans, and English kept a middle course. They admitted pictures and images; but denied them *every kind* of worship. However, it may be asserted, without hazard of contradiction, that the clergy universally agreed in one *kind of idolatry. Before the image of power, with the purse of the state in it's hand, they all bowed, prostituted themselves, and sacrificed their people, their conscience, and their religion,* if any such they had.

At a council, or rather parliament, of Northumberland, in 787, several *decent* canons were made, respecting the character and duty of the clergy, and the harmony that should be preserved among the people. One of them enacts, that the people, in the eucharist, shall offer a whole loaf, and not a bare crust; which casts some light on the customs of the country, on that occasion.

The last question, publicly discussed in councils, was "Whether Christ, as to his human nature, was the *natural* and *proper,* or only the *adoptive,* son of God." After the discussion of several western councils, the former was declared to be the *orthodox* doctrine.

These extracts, it is hoped, will justify the character given of these two ages, as effectually as they go to establish the fact, "that the ignorance, ambition, licentiousness, and venality of the clergy, have no small share of popular ignorance, superstition and vice, to account for."

The ninth age preserves all the characters of the two former, and in their darkest colours. Besides, it introduces new subjects of wrangling and discord, whose folly and unimportance, to say no worse, the christian world has not yet got wisdom or honesty enough to reject, expose, and reprobate. Such are predestination, grace, *as then represented*, the real presence in the eucharist, and some others. A few extracts will be sufficient to present the characters of the disputants, on these subjects, and that of the times.

During the first part of this century, image-worship was still the great subject of discussion. In the east, emperors discouraged it; empresses, like Irene, were uniformly it's patronesses. In France, it was warmly contested, both in word and writing, and, finally, was established.

About the year 845, Gotteschaleus, a French monk, broached the doctrine of the "predestination of the saints to glory, and of the wicked to damnation." At the first mention of the idea, alarm, horror, and execration, were, almost universally felt and expressed. Early in the disputes on this subject, Gotteschaleus defined the divine decree, in both its objects, as, "*immutable*," *and extending to the impossibility of repentance, in the wicked, because of the opposing decree of God.*

This doctrine was condemned by the council of Mentz, in 848, *as wicked and pernicious.* And the council of Quiercy, added to this sentence, the deposition, scourging, and perpetual imprisonment of its author.

About this time the doctrine of the "real presence," was first agitated. It was introduced and asserted by Paschosius, abbot of Corby: and denied by most of the learned of the age; if "learned" any of them may be called. Most of them wrote upon the subject; and their writings form a mass of mystical nonsense, if not impiety. The agitation of this subject introduced several foolish, and even dirty and obscene questions; such as, whether the flesh and blood of Christ, into which the bread and wine in the eucharist was supposed to be changed, suffer digestion, and pass into excrement? and that " de partu Virginis." Concerning the former, the western church gravely admitted, that no part of (what they called) the mystical flesh and blood, passed into excrement; but, that the whole was either *annihilated*, or changed into *our* flesh to *form our resurrection bodies*. About the latter question there was much writing, and variety of opinion. Some maintained that Christ came into the world, non " per virginalis januam vulvæ, sed monstruose de secreto ventris incerto tramite." Others, and among the rest, the famous Bertramn, or Ratrumn, asserted that this was, " non nasci sed erumpi;" and Bertram published a treatise, in which he maintained that Christ came into the world " per semitam vulvæ;" but that Mary, notwithstanding, continued a virgin, " ante-partum, in partu, & post partum;" he having come into the world " per vulvam clausum," as he afterwards entered the room where his disciples were, through a shut door. This delicate treatise, which such of my readers as understand Latin, must admire, was dedicated to the abbess and nuns of Soissons. To such as do not, I can only say, that delicacy forbids the translation of the Latin phrases, which I have quoted. I wish the object of this little abstract would have allowed me to omit the quotation. But we ought to see, not only *men*, but *bishops*, in their true colours. Men of God! while ye appear in such colours, what must be the complexion of the untaught and deluded people! Can any thing be expected but the darkest tints of ignorance, absurdity, superstition, and sin!

The only circumstance which can be adduced to shed a ray of light on the gloomy picture of this age, is the injunction of some councils, in France and Italy, to *erect schools in all cathedral churches*, for *teaching the liberal sciences*, and Music. However, even the brightness of this ray is obscured by the fact, that they were only for the education of the *existing priests*; and the branches to be taught, scarcely deserve the name of " science." Yet feeble as the spark was, and long smothered, it gathered strength afterwards, and latterly spread a wonderful blaze of knowledge over the greater part of Europe.

In this century popes and antipopes make their appearance, thundering bulls, one against another. During the last eighteen years, pope succeeded pope, with wonderful rapidity. No less than eight appear upon the stage. Of these one brought the emperor to Rome to behead his opponents. A successor digs up his body, gives it a mock trial, strips it of the pontifical habit, cuts off its fingers, and throws it into the Tyber. At the same time he annuls all his decrees and acts, and has his barbarity approved by a *synod* at Rome. His immediate successor, in like manner, annulled all *his* decrees, and, a few years after, John 9th, in council, confirmed the last annulment, condemned the acts of the barbarous Stephen to the fire, and excommunicated those who had dug up and mangled the body of Formosus.

What a scene is here! But it is not to be considered as peculiarly acted by "Popes." After ages—ay! and ages boasting of more extensive knowledge, manners more civilized, and principles more liberal, have, long since, acted the same, *over and over*. And, wherever the clergy look to the rulers of the state, for " DISTINCTION and EMOLUMENT," it will be acted *over and over again*, to the end of the chapter. Even, in the convulsions of states, and the horrors of insurrection, where either mercy arrests the sword of justice; or justice, sensible that she has been imposed on, withdraws her restraints, her terrors, and her precautionary inflictions; nay, where she has honorably reconducted the objects of her suspicion to their families and friends, and restored them to freedom, honor, and the blessings of society; the rancour of a jealous, mean, and *venal clergy*, will *usurp even the power of state, slander, rob,* and *persecute man, woman, and child—widow and orphan*—provided there remain one vile minion of a ruling faction, to approve their villainies, and through whom they expect the meanest gratification of their avarice or ambition. At this moment, my boding mind looks forward, with horror, to the commencement of the nineteenth century. There, methinks, I see an isle, fair, fertile, and salubrious, as the garden of God; long famed for it's science and sanctity; and, latterly, blessed with the introduction of a church, whose standard is the bible, whose forms are modest simplicity, and whose discipline is nearly apostolical! There, I see the successors of persecuted saints, who shewed their willingness " to spend and be spent," in the cause of religious truth and religious liberty, basely hunting after promotion, bartering the independence of Christ's freemen for the paltry emoluments of Mammon's slaves, volunteering as political spies and inquisitors, and proscribing their brethren.—Nay, forgetful of the short, but imperative commission, received by the apostles from their divine master, "*go and teach all nations;*" I see them, erecting a barrier around the church of Christ, and saying, " thus far shalt thou extend, but no farther!" Should burning zeal for truth and virtue carry her arms beyond our boundaries, he must support the warfare at his own charge. He may go forth with " the sword of the spirit, which is the word of God." —He may " put on the breastplate of righteousness," use, as " an helmit, the hope of salvation," with " the shield of faith, he may quench the fiery darts of the wicked," and have " his feet shod with the preparation of the gospel of peace." Thus accoutred, he may go forth, in the spirit of ancient prophets, and primitive apostles, " conquering and to conquer" the ignorance, errors, prejudices, vanities, and vices of the world ; and we wish him, " GOD SPEED ! But, as in his romantic attempts to extend—to universalize—the kingdom of God, and of *his* Christ, *we* have disclaimed all participation, in the bounties of *our* king, and of *our* LORD, *he* shall have no share."

Is this a dream ? Is it a communication from above? Or, is it a suggestion of Satan, to alarm my apprehensions, and depress my spirits ? Be still, my heart ! The lenient hand of God shall soothe thy pains, and time, in his progress, resolve thy doubts !

In this age, the manners of the clergy had become more depraved than ever, as appears from the numerous and severe canons, for their restraint or reformation. Should it be alleged that the number and severity of these acts go to exempt the clergy, as a body, from the charge of depravity, an answer immediately presents itself. These canons were not the acts of councils, merely ecclesiastical ; but of mixed assemblies, where princes presided, and the laity made a part ; and many of them, particularly in France, were enacted by the *civil power alone.*

The writers of this century produced nothing valuable.

Ignorance had fostered superstition almost to maturity. Superstition produced a gloomy, austere, and mortified sanctimony. Every wrongheaded enthusiast was dubbed a saint; and every saint found a panegyrist, as wrongheaded as himself. Relics came into vogue. Bits of rotten wood or bone became objects, both of worship and traffick; whose value was enhanced by forged miracles. Hence, fabulous legends, of discoveries, of tombs, of visions, and lying wonders, were the spawn of, almost, every pen; and the ignorant, deluded and credulous multitude swallowed, with avidity, their monstrous progeny. Indulgences began to creep out, but with a rarity and diffidence, which shewed their fear of meeting the eye of common sense, darkened as it was; and, in some countries, tithes were extended from the produce of the soil, to that of labor and honest industry.

The tenth century has been called by most authors, the age of "darkness, ignorance, and obscurity." And it cannot be denied, that ignorance and irregularity were more general, and extended farther, both among clergy and people, than at any former period.

In the last, the court had become licentious, and the clergy as imperious and profligate, and as violent persecutors of each other, as their brethren in the west. In the pursuit of preferment and wealth, patriarchs, at Constantinople, exhibit the same scenes of mutual persecution, deposition, and banishment, which popes acted at Rome. Religion rapidly declined, and the Greek church was as unproductive, as the Roman, of good men, or learned authors.

During the first thirty-five years, the succession of popes was rapid, and their character infamous. So glaring were their enormities, that they could not be concealed; and so horrid, that even Bellarmin exclaims, "How frightful, at that time, was the face of the church! The holy see was fallen under the tyranny of two licentious women, who placed and displaced bishops, as their humour led them, and seated their gallants in St. Peter's chair." The state of Rome continued nearly the same to the end of this century. The popes were openly guilty of perjury, murder, sacrilege, incest, and every other crime which can render humanity odious or execrable.

Yet, so depraved were the clergy, that even the worst of them had *synods* to support them, while they could retain their power. Indeed, if we believe Ratherius, bishop of Verona, the Italian clergy, at this time, were as irregular, immodest, and licentious, as ever disgraced the name. Speaking of them, he says: "If they do not confess their sins, they are in danger of damnation; and, if they do, the canons exclude them from the discharge of their functions; so that the church would be without ministers, the number of the wicked is so great."

The ignorance of the clergy is evident, from the qualifications requisite to ordination; viz. to be able to repeat the creed and the Lord's prayer; to read, distinctly, the gospel and epistles; to know how to administer baptism, penance, and extreme unction; to perform the ceremonies of the burial of the dead; and of blessing the holy water; to be well versed in singing, and in the calendar; and to have a martyrology and penitential.

In France, notwithstanding the distraction of the times, arising from political contests, division of the country into three kingdoms, the succession of the Capets to the throne, &c. learning, religion, and the clergy had a better aspect. Philosophy and mathematics were studied by some. Gubert, archbishop of Rheims, and afterwards pope, composed several tracts of rhetoric and geometry. He knew the use of telescopes; invented clocks; and constructed a sphere. There were also a few others who studied in the same line, and even directed their attention to astronomy. But, whatever superiority this gave France over Italy, still the sphere of knowledge was contracted, and learning rare. It is observable also, that the French clergy were less irregular, their superstition less absurd, and the people less corrupted and enslaved. The infallibility of popes, and consequently, their absolute supremacy, was rejected with spirit; and a semblance of freedom preserved in the Gallican councils. Monkery, however, gained ground; and monks becoming haughty, were looked on, by the clergy, with a jealous eye.

In Germany, the state of the church was still more favorable. It may even be said to have been flourishing. The piety and valor of its emperors, the respectability of its bishops, and the good sense of several writers, were all in it's favor; and christianity, *such as it then was,* extended it's empire among the northern nations. The clergy, as a body, seem to have been free from the general and gross irregularities, elsewhere prevalent, and attentive to their duty. Hence, the people were more rational and religious.

Early in the preceding century, Alfred restored the universities in England, brought over learned men from France, and zealously encouraged the liberal arts and sciences. His successors directed their principal attention to the reformation of the manners of the clergy, and the discipline of the church. The rules enacted by Edward, in the beginning of the tenth century, against the disturbers of the church, apostates, sabbath breakers, sorcerors, lewd women, persons guilty of incest, and *clergymen, who commit fornication and robbery*, prove the degeneracy of the clergy, and the depravity of the people. Most of these were re-enacted by Ethelstan, who succeeded him, in the year 923. He also issued regulations for the trial of persons accused, by fire or water, called "ordeal." As this circumstance is curious, and, generally, little known; and, as it casts light on the character of the times, I transcribe the following account of it. "Let the person, desirous of clearing himself by the trial of fire, or water, come to the priest three days before, who shall give him a benediction in the usual form. During those three days let him eat nothing, but bread and salt, or pulse, hear mass every day, and make an oblation. On the day of trial, let him receive the sacrament. If the trial be by cold water, let him be plunged one fathom below the surface: if by hot, let it be boiling, and the hand or arm put into it. If by hot iron, let it be put into his hand for three days, without looking on it. In all these trials, both the accused and the accuser are to fast, and to have twelve witnesses present, who may take an oath with them; and let holy water be sprinkled on them." What superstition and barbarism are here!

In the year 967, king Edgar, by direction of St. Dunstan, being more *religious* than his predecessors, not only published similar laws, but re-established what was then called, "*the purity of discipline in the church.*" What that discipline was may be judged of by the subjects of the laws. These were, "the preservation of the revenues of the church, the payment of tithes and Peter's pence, the solemn observation of Sundays and *festivals*, the celebration of mass, confession, penances, &c. &c. As to those laws, which related to the *manners* and *morals* of the clergy, they seem to have been equally necessary and wise.

To give efficacy to the latter, Edgar gave a commission to Dunstan, archbishop of canterbury, Ethelwold bishop of Winchester, and Oswald of Worcester, with power, not only to censure and repress the irregularity and insolence of the clergy, but to turn the dissolute out of their churches, and substitute others in their place.

In virtue of this commission, Dunston held a general council in England, in the year 973, in which he published decrees for the *expulsion* of the *dissolute* clergy, and the *compulsion* of the *whole body* to embrace a monastic life, or to retire. Soon after, he and his two colleagues turned the *greater number* of the clergy out of their churches for their immoralities, and put monks in their place; and compelled the rest to assume a monastic habit. The consequence proved, that there are few things more difficult than reforming the morals of a *dissolute clergy;* or restraining the spirit of *covetous, proud,* and *ambitious priests,* of any denomination, or in any age. Those excluded by Dunstan, became querulous, seditious, and turbulent, even attempting force, not only to recover their churches, but to take possession of the monasteries, lately founded. Dunstan, however, maintained his *reform* with firmness and success. And it is but justice to observe, that he was not more severe in his reformation of discipline, and correction of profligate churchmen, than he was bold and zealous in his censures of royal debauchery, and lordly contempt of the laws of the church. He put king Edgar, his patron, under a seven years penance for chusing a maid whom he had sent for out of a monastery: and, in *opposition both to king and pope,* he kept a *powerful lord* under excommunication, till he submitted to penance, and prostrated himself before him in a council, barefooted, clothed in a woollen garment, holding a bundle of rods in his hand, and lamenting his sin. He is said, also, to have been friendly to the revival and study of liberal science.

In this century there were no controversies about articles of faith, or theological doctrines. The people were so besotted, that one party swallowed *implicitly* whatever their preachers *vomited* from the pulpit: the other abandoned themselves to the grossest sensualities, and the gratification of their brutal appetites.

On the whole, this was the age, not only of darkness, but of stupidity, licentiousness, and discord. The veneration for the See of Rome was universal; but the personal wickedness of the popes, which rendered their characters odious, prevented any great accession to their power. As yet they were not absolute sovereigns, even of Rome; though they had great demesnes in Italy, granted by Pepin, and, afterwards, confirmed by the Emperors.

Councils were, comparatively, few: and their decrees, as already mentioned, related to tithes, revenues, *churchmen*, and *concubines*. In some instances, pluralities appear, and ordination of minor *peerlings* to the richer bishopricks. The benediction of bells was introduced; and the office of the Virgin Mary, began to be recited, as a part of divine service. The first formal and solemn canonization of a SAINT was likewise reserved for this age.

The eleventh century, though itself dark, promises the approach of returning day to the intellectual and moral world. Though many new disputes arose about the ceremonies and services of religion—though episcopal pride sprung up, to an alarming height—though monachism spread it's dark domain—though clerical irregularity, licentiousness, and rapacity, still abounded—and, though popes arrogated the sovereign dominion of the earth, in addition to that of heaven and hell—intellect began to be exercised, and reason acquired boldness to discuss principles, rights, and duties; and, though in the progress of ages, this led to the happy restoration of learning, science, and religion, in the beginning, it only multiplied difficulties, doubts, and absurdities.

In this century, Fulbert bishop of Chartres, first claims our attention, being deemed one of the principal restorers of learning, the sciences, and divinity. His fame brought scholars from all parts, who, as the French historians say, left him, replete with knowledge and piety, and became conspicuous luminaries both in France and Germany. However, the extracts from his writings give no very high idea, either of his parts or attainments. Mysticism every where appears. His views of baptism exhibit perfect silliness; and the sacrament of the Eucharist he represents as equally sublime and *incomprehensible.* All his other writings are about tithes, revenues, ceremonies, &c. and, therefore, I shall pass him by, without farther notice.

About the middle of this century, the question of the " *real presence*" revived by Berenger, a disciple of Fulbert, and arch-deacon of Angers, was much agitated. Berenger was condemned by several councils, regularly recanted, and as regularly relapsed. Many of the most eminent men of the time wrote against him, particularly Lanfranc, archbishop of Canterbury, a zealous stickler for the " real presence." Some also dared to write in his favor; however, their reasonings, on both sides, are childish, fanciful, and absurd. To retail them would be equally so. Yet, a sketch of their notions, on this subject, may be both entertaining and useful. The terms in which Berenger signed his recantations, may be placed, with justice, in the front of this sketch, as they were prescribed by councils, holden in Rome, in the years 1055 and 1078. " I believe in my heart," says he, " and confess with my mouth, that the bread and wine, upon the altar, are *substantially* changed, by the *mystery* of the *priest,* and the words of our Saviour into the *true, proper,* and *quickening* body and blood of our Lord Jesus Christ, which came out of his side; which I swear by the HOLY and CONSUBSTANTIAL TRINITY, and by the holy Evangelists." The word " mystery," here used, deserves particular attention. In the original, it signifies " a secret," or any thing not known or understood, merely because not revealed, or explained. Hence, in the sixteenth and seventeenth century, it was applied in the English language, to every art, or trade, where education or instruction was necessary, *brogue-making not excepted.* From this, the phrase " mystery of the priest," requires no explanation. Whatever difficulty the reader may find in affixing a determinate idea to the word " quickening, as applied by Berenger, it will not be removed by Lanfranc. " We believe," says he, " that the terrestrial substances, sanctified at the holy table, by *the divine efficacy and ministry of the priests*, are converted, after an *ineffable*, *incomprehensible*, and *miraculous* manner, by the *operation* of *the supreme power*, into the essential body of our Saviour, lest MEN SHOULD BE STRUCK WITH HORROR, IF THEY WERE TO EAT RAW AND BLOODY FLESH; AND THAT THEY, BELIEVING WHAT THEY DID NOT SEE, MIGHT MERIT THE GREATER REWARD: that, notwithstanding this, the *body of Jesus Christ is still in heaven, immortal, entire, without defect, and impassible;* so that we may truly say, " WE DO, AND DO NOT, receive the same body, which was born of the virgin; because, *it is the same,* with respect to the essence, propriety, and efficacy, of it's nature; and, *it is not the same,* when we consider the appearances of bread and wine, and the other qualities." So much of his grace. Guitmond, a French archbishop, went beyond *even* him. He maintained " that though the host be divided into several parts, the body of Christ is not divided, but remains whole, entire, and the same, under each wafer: and, though in the hands of a thousand priests, who say mass in different places, is still in heaven—that the consecrated bread cannot be gnawn by vermin, consumed by fire, or corrupted; but only *appears* to be so, as a *punishment of human infidelity*:—that the bread and wine are not necessarily changed into the body and blood of Christ, except among those *who have faith to believe this mystery*—and, that, would any heretic prevail on a priest to consecrate one or more great loaves to try, whether, when eaten, they should be turned to excrement, they would not; or rather that God would permit such heretic to be deceived, by ordering some angel, or other spirit, to steal away the consecrated bread, and put unconsecrated in its place." Surely, more is unnecessary on this subject.

The popes of this age, with scarcely one exception, were not only worthless, but wicked. Contentions about the papal chair, and cotemporary popes, appear more than once. In the year 1073, Hildebrand was advanced to that dignity, and assumed the name of Gregory 7th. On his promotion, he instantly conceived the vast design of being supreme Lord, both spiritual and temporal, over all the earth. Every thing was favorable to his pre-

pretensions. Germany was weak; France governed by a child; England newly conquered by the Normans; Spain, partly, in the hands of the Moors; the kingdoms of the North newly converted; Italy torn into patches by a great number of petty princes; and all Europe split into parties. This general state of affairs Gregory turned to his own advantage, with great address. During the twelve years of his papacy, he was unremitting in his exertions; and his success was great as his ambition was towering. His temporal dominion was greatly extended, and he affected to rule most of the churches as his own diocess. He projected croisades, which were afterwards executed by his successors. Victor 3d sent 100,000 men into Africa; and Urban 2d, his successor, got a vast army mustered, and dispatched to the same quarter, under the command of several princes, for the purpose of recovering the holy land from the Turks.

The breach between the Latin and Greek churches became incurable, through the immoderate insolence of the pope's legates, and the ambition of Cerularius, patriarch of Constantinople. The matters in dispute were beneath the notice of reasonable beings; such as, " the shaving of beards, the use of leavened, or unleavened bread in the eucharist," and the like. The more moderate Greeks were most offended by foisting the words " *filioque*" (and the son) into the western creeds. In these disputes, the substance of religion was lost, while the clergy were worrying each other about the shadow. Cardinal Humbert, the pope's legate, concluded his part in the affray, by " declaring Cerularius, his followers and abettors, anathematized, with all other heretics, or rather, with *the devil and his angels*, if they did not repent. And this pious sentence he pronounced " in the name of the *holy trinity*, of the *apostolic see*, of the ORTHODOX *fathers*, the *seven councils*, and the *whole Catholic church*."

Peter Damien, cardinal bishop of Ostia, made a considerable figure, soon after the middle of this century. His writings contain much good sense, but not unmixed with fooleries. He reprobated all wars, interference of the civil power, and infliction of civil penalties, on account of religion; and maintained " that every man's soul shall appear, at the day of judgment, in the same state wherein it left the body." At the same time, he is said to have been the first proposer of *voluntary whipping* for sins of the flesh; and of vicarious penance.

As to the peace which the churches of England enjoyed, during the life of Dunstan, it died with him. The country was overrun by babarians; churches were pillaged and razed, monasteries ruined, and Canterbury consumed by fire. Civil wars between Edward, and Godwin earl of Kent, with his son Harold, and a general corruption of manners followed; and the death of the Confessor, without issue, completed the national ruin. In 1066, William of Normandy, having killed the usurper Harold, subdued the country, and established new laws, civil and ecclesiastical. He forbade his subjects to acknowledge any pope, or receive any bulls from Rome, *without his leave*: nor would he suffer the archbishop of Canterbury, to make any constitutions, *except such as he approved;* or any excommunications to be issued against his subjects, *without his orders.* Lanfranc, however, espoused the cause of Rome, and supported her claims, during the whole of William's reign.

On his death, his son, William 2d (Rufus) caused all the church revenues to be registered, computed a maintenance for the monks, reunited the overplus to the demesnes of the crown, and farmed them, yearly, to the highest bidder: and, in order to secure an absolute power over the church, when bishops died, he kept their sees vacant. Canterbury was so for five years, till, in a fit of sickness, superstition waving her gloomy banner, induced him to send for Anselm, a Norman monk, whom he promoted to that see. Anselm, however, disappointed him. He was inflexibly attached to Rome, and maintained a continual struggle with William and Henry 1st, till his death in 1109.

In France and Flanders, some opinions, deemed heretical, were holden, in the beginning of this century, and the authors punished with death. Among others, the following are recorded: "that baptism did not procure the remission of sins; that the consecration of the priest does not constitute the sacrament of the eucharist; and that prayers to martyrs and confessors, were of no use." The persons accused of these were charged with some horrid practices, which deserved death. But the charges appear in a shape truly questionable. In Flanders, on examination, the culprits acknowledged the following doctrines: " That, provided they practised the precepts of the gospel, renounced the vanities of the world, and the gratification of their passions, earned their livelihood honestly, did no injury, and exercised charity, baptism was unnecessary; that, if these duties were neglected, baptism would not profit; and, that though at first, it might have had some efficacy, it was then useless, for three reasons: 1st, *the profligacy of the clergy*; 2d, the after-sins of the baptised; and 3d, because infants baptised, who have neither faith nor free-will, who neither know the meaning of these words, nor desire baptism, *cannot receive any benefit from the profession of others.*" The holders of these opinions are said to have been convinced of their errors, by the *piety* and eloquence of a bishop, and, by recantation, to have saved their lives. Be that as it may, we may see, in the opinions themselves, the seeds that vegetated afterwards, spread their branches far and wide, and grew up to the *reformation* of which we boast.

Several French councils prohibited clergymen from carrying arms, or going to war, and deprived of benefice and dignity, such as did

In most of the councils of this age, little appears, except what goes to prove the prevalence of simony and debauchery among the clergy, and the gross ignorance, superstition, licentiousness, and barbarity of the people—the natural consequence, and unavoidable effect of the former. Clerical learning, in general, was comprised in the knowledge of " the psalter, hymns, canticles, epistles, gospels, and prayers." Nor are ye to suppose that this implied the understanding, or capacity of expounding them. No such thing! It was only the knowledge of what psalms, hymns, epistles, gospels, and prayers, were to be used on each sunday and holiday.

The ecclesiastical and theological works, of this age are few, and of no value. The historical are mere legends and romances, in honor of favorite saints. Of the Greek writers little better can be said. Scarcely a vestige of their ancient genius, learning, or spirit, can be traced. One specimen will be sufficient to give an idea, both of their literary and religious character. It is taken from Simeon, an abbot, who was of great repute, as a writer, about the end of this century. "Three things are necessary," says he, "in order to attain the objects of your desire; viz. the contempt of all creatures, rational and irrational, mortification, and a pure conscience, free from passion and interest. Afterwards, sitting alone in tranquillity, in the corner of your cell, do what I am now about to tell you. Keeping your door shut, lift your mind above all vanities, and, bowing your head *to your belly*, hold your breath: seek your heart in mind. At first you will find thick darkness, but by continuing this practice day and night, you will discover wonders, and find endless consolation. For, when the mind has once discovered the seat of the soul, it clearly perceives things which it never comprehended before. It discerns air all around the heart, and becomes quite luminous and full of wisdom. And when a man is arrived at that height of perfection, if any evil thought intervene, it is expelled before it can make any impression; so that the mind, being exasperated, drives away the devil. Ye may learn the rest with God, by preserving Jesus Christ in your heart." However transcendent this may appear to minds not altogether lost to rationality, it is *plain sense*, compared with what he has written about "Divine Lights and Illuminations, essential unions with God, impressions of the elements upon human souls, and the uncreated and eternal light of the divine majesty, as seen on mount Tabor." If such was the higher, what must the lower order of Greek writers have been, at this period!

Though the literary character was generally low, some began, latterly, to study divinity *rationally*, and discuss theological questions *logically*, but to no great purpose.

As to discipline, it began to relax. The frequency of excommunications rendered them contemptible. Pilgrimages, absolutions, vicarious penance, the whip, and croisades, were all in fashion. Monachism made great strides towards wealth and power; and several new orders were instituted. Still, however, the great body of the clergy continued illiterate and immoral; and, consequently, the people remained in ignorance, superstition, and sin. The few individuals, which arose, with more learning and goodness, may be rather considered as scattered sparks of light in an atmosphere beset with darkness, which only serve to render it visible, and expose the deformity of superstition's phantoms, than luminaries to direct and cheer the weary traveller in the path of religious science, to her temple and her treasures.

The twelfth century, however, presents us with better writers, and more information; yet the number of the former was small, and the sum of the latter trifling, compared with the multitude of weak and foolish scribblers, and the mass of ignorance and superstition, every where remaining.

The church in some countries, had nearly attained a plenitude of power, at the beginning of this age; yet did not presume to claim the right of judging ecclesiastics, in cases affecting life, but delivered them over to the civil magistrate. In affairs, however, merely ecclesiastical, the clergy inflexibly supported what they deemed their rights, not only by arguments, but by arms. In France, though the churches were endowed by government, all interference of the crown was rejected, both in the choice and ordination of the clergy. The interference and influence of the popes, however, were not so easily guarded against. As, on every difference, appeals to Rome were encouraged, the pontiffs acquired a great share in the collection of benefices. For, though the bishops were chosen by the clergy, and ordained by the metropolitan; yet, on every dispute about the validity of an election, the decision must be referred to the consistory of Rome, where the popes had absolute power to nominate their own favorites; and if the metropolitan refused ordination, they performed the rite themselves. They also claimed the right of investiture, which involved them, not only in disputes, but wars, with kings and emperors. Rival candidates for the papal chair, were very frequent at this time. Four antipopes appeared in a few years; and, during a great part of that time, the powers of the continent were almost equally divided between two of them, Gregory (Innocent 2d) and Peter of Leon.

In the writings of Ivo, bishop of Chartres, a man of good dispositions, considerable parts, and no contemptible erudition, for the time, we find many things well worth attention. He was zealous for the reformation of the discipline of the church, and the manners of the clergy. But the character of the times, and the jealousies of kings and popes, exposed him to great difficulties, in many cases. His zeal for discipline, was frequently checked by his love of peace, and fear of exciting discord, by giving offence to the civil power. One instance will present a sketch of his character. Great disorders had crept into the diocess of Sens, and thefts had been committed on the goods of the church. The archbishop, as appears, was pressed by the king to restore the culprits, without penance, or restitution, and applied to Ivo, for advice, how to conduct himself. Ivo concludes a very sensible letter, on his friend's dilemma, between the mandate of the king, and the canons of the church, by prescribing the following form, with a remark annexed: " Do not deceive yourselves : I admit you into the visible church, notwithstanding the crimes of which you are guilty: but I cannot open to you the gates of the kingdom of heaven; and, therefore, I absolve you no further than I have power; those of more courage and piety may find better methods in such cases." This, adds he, to his friend, seems to me proper enough : not that I hereby prescribe to others, but think it best to prevent farther mischief to the church, by submitting thus far to the necessity of the times.

Several opinions, deemed heretical, sprung from, or were revived by the infantine discussions of this age, and became popular, viz. " that baptism was of no use to infants ; that crosses should not be worshipped ; that the mass was useless ; that alms and prayers for the dead, are of no avail ; that no trust should be placed in the mediation of saints ; that all the usages of the church, *not established by Jesus Christ and his apostles*, are superstitious ; that a purgatory has no existence ; and that souls departed, passed immediately into the place, and state, allotted for them." These doctrines were received, with such avidity, in France, that, in several provinces, the churches were nearly deserted. They spread through Flanders with a reception equally favorable, and even reached Rome.

The accounts given of those who published, or embraced these doctrines, is the most absurd, extravagant, and improbable, that can be conceived. But these ac-

E

counts are given by enemies, ignorant, illiterate, preju-
diced, jealous, and provoked; who mixed a thousand
fooleries, misrepresentations, and calumnies with a few
shades of truth. Yet all these conspire to lead the rational mind to conclusions, of which they were little aware.
It would be of no use to copy their overcharged, fantas-
tical, and ridiculous portraits of these people. Let a short
extract from that of Herbert, a co-temporary *monk*, and not
the weakest, or most wicked, of those who wrote to expose
them, stand for the whole. " There are," says he, " a
great many heretics in the county of Perigueux, who eat
no flesh, drink no wine, fall on their knees an hundred
times a day, and *receive no money*. They bear no regard
to the mass, adore no crosses, but accuse, of idolatry,
those who do so. This sect is mightily encreased. Not
only great numbers of persons of quality, forsake their
estates to join them, but a great many ecclesiastics, and
religious of both sexes, follow them. The most stupid
and senseless among them, in less than eight days time,
become very expert, apt to teach, and be examplars to
others. It is a hard matter to take them, for, wherever
they are apprehended, the devil releases them from prison.
They work some miracles, such as filling a vessel with
wine, by pouring some drops of water into it."

It is impossible to pass this memoir without a few
slight remarks. First, their devotion, mortification, and
contempt of riches are fully admitted. Secondly, Their
characters and abilities not only attracted ecclesiastics,
monks, and nuns, in spite of their prejudices, but induced nobles to abandon their property, and, no doubt,
their connexions, to espouse their cause. Thirdly, Their
eloquence so far eclipsed that of the bishops and priests,
and even the *indulgential* sanctity of the monks, as
to leave their churches without people, if we may believe
another account, given by the famous St. Bernard.
Fourthly, Their converts must have been comparatively
sensible and well-informed, who, by eight days addition-
al instruction among them, could become capable of
teaching, so as to produce such effects. Fifthly, Their
being released from prison by the devil, and, at the same
time, working miracles, has an odd appearance. Surely,
their release, and miracle-working power, must have

both proceeded from the devil; or fellowship between God and Belial must be admitted. The fact, however, seems to have been simply this. They were the most religious, sensible, and well-informed people of their time, and therefore hated by the clergy. In Italy they were so numerous, powerful, and zealous, that they raised formidable insurrections against the popes, Eugenius 3d, and Adrian 4th. The latter laid the whole people of Rome under excommunication, till they should expel them. Superstition was alarmed, took up arms, and drove them into Tuscany, where they were kindly received. From this time they were condemned by synods and persecuted by princes, under the name of Albigenses. Thirty of them are said to have fled to England, where they were apprehended, condemned by an assembly of bishops, branded on the cheek with a red hot iron, by order of Henry 2d, publicly whipped, driven out of Oxford half-naked, and starved to death.

Surprising as this success, and pitiable as the fate of these worthy people may appear, the cause of that success, and consequently of their fate, as stated by Lewis du Pin, who cannot be suspected of partiality to them, is not less melancholy and mortifying. Though he does not express himself with much precision, his language is intelligible, and, alas! too true. "The relaxation of church discipline," says he, " *the covetousness of the clergy,* the common abuse made of the sacraments, the ignorance and credulity of the people, the pretended virtues of these new preachers, and the desire of reformation, were the causes of the amazing progress of these upstart opinions." Take this in connexion with what he admits elsewhere, and arrange the matter under the eye of common sense, and the statement will stand thus: " The *profligacy and covetousness of the clergy* had outrun the feelings of the people; and their fables, their credulity; so that the desire of reformation had been excited. The simplicity, self-denial, and other virtues of the new preachers, recommended them as reformers, and their good sense, rationality, and unaffected zeal for truth and virtue, gave currency to their doctrine, and credit to their name."

During the papacy of Adrian 4th, (five years) several remarkable circumstances occurred. Among these his *famous* letter to Henry 2d, of England, mentioned by Matthew Paris, investing him with authority to *subdue, occupy,* and *enjoy Ireland,* is not the least remarkable. The authenticity of the grant is, by some, doubted. But, be that as it may, authentic or non-authentic, it has been the same to Ireland ; and, by the meanness and venality of a faction, is the same still. Ireland, said to be incorporated, is only provincialized ; she is *actually possessed,* as a province ; whether she will ever be *enjoyed,* as such, depends on the *wisdom* of future British councils. To that wisdom, at present, there is no pretensions. Apostates, in fact, can have no wisdom. They know their honesty is questionable ; and, to patch up its appearance, they have recourse to fury, and the persecution of the persons and principles which they have basely betrayed ; and, in betraying which, posterity will feel that they have been equally traitors to the king, who clothes them with honors, and the country which feeds them.

In this century flourished the learned, indiscreet, persecuted, and abused Peter Abelard, and his equally sensible, indiscreet, and pitiable Heloissa, whose fame will live, while English poetry shall be read. Pity it is, that the genius of a Pope has not shaded their foibles, by throwing more light on virtues, which cannot be denied them. In England, the contests between Henry 2d, and Thomas Becket, archbishop of Canterbury, were frequent and interesting. At one time they promised a total separation from the See of Rome. Though this did not take place, the articles of Clarendon, in 1164, greatly reduced the papal power, by subjecting ecclesiastical courts, revenues, and demesnes to the courts of law, and control of the crown.

Becket, who had signed these articles, was induced, by the murmurs and remonstrances of those about him, to retract, and enter upon a voluntary penance, till pope Alexander 3d, gave him absolution, on his confessing to a priest.

This tergiversation of Becket enraged Henry. Becket, aware of his violent temper, endeavoured to escape to France ; but being twice disappointed, he returned to Canterbury, and presented himself before the king, by whom he was harshly treated, yet would not submit.

Henry sent an embassy to the pope, demanding that the archbishop of York might be constituted legate; that the customs and privileges of the kingdom might be confirmed by the See of Rome; and that Becket, and the other bishops might be enjoined to conform to them.

The pope, in some measure, granted the first; but refused the other two. The king determined to proceed against Becket, summoned him to appear before him. He pleaded his dignity in excuse for not appearing before a secular judge. The king, exasperated by this excuse, called an assembly of lords spiritual and temporal, at Northampton, who pronounced sentence against him as contumacious; and, afterwards, to indulge the king's resentment, pronounced him a *perjured traitor*. Wherever covetousness or ambition have an end to serve with princes, or any other vile passion has the ruin of an honest man in view, the charge of treason is a ready, sharp, and formidable weapon. The moment it is taken up, fools are alarmed; dependants, sycophants, and parasites, seem to tremble for the prince or state; mock-loyalty raises the hue and cry; and nothing is heard of but proscriptions, prisons, banishment, halters, and hatchets, with the unhalowed hallooings of a black battalion in full cry after *bounty*, and *regardless* of character or *blood*. Yet, in the present instance, though these *holy* and *loyal* bishops were keen set, they dared not to bring Becket to a formal trial. No! they were afraid of the issue; and they knew their purpose would be as *effectually*, and more surely served, by *defamation, slander*, and *secession*. *The good men*, therefore, went no farther than sending him a civil message, " *that, as he was a perjured traitor*, they did not consider themselves bound to obey him."

After this, he refused again to be judged by the king, bishops, and other lords; and having reason to fear assassination, he retired into France, where he was kindly received by Lewis 7th; and afterwards, he experienced the like kindness from the pope, who made him legate of all England, except the province of York. The remainder of his life was a continual scene of persecution, debate, and negociation with the king; till he was assassinated before the altar, in the cathedral of Canterbury, by four of Henry's courtiers, in 1170, which was the fifty-second year of his age. Of this vile transaction Henry does not appear to have been innocent. Be that as it may, Becket was canonized as a saint, and Henry, alarmed by the rebellion of his son, did homage to his memory, by going barefooted to his tomb, in all the meanness of crest-fallen pride, and folly of superstition, and devoutly imploring his assistance.

What a motely, melancholy and humiliating scene is here exhibited! Yet, withdraw the name of king, the crime of assassination, and the idea of saintship, and one would be tempted to suspect that it was acted among ourselves, within the last five years, by a body of men, calling themselves *ministers of the gospel*, and not by bishops of the 12th century.

The writings of this age exhibit many pictures, nearly of the same class. Bishops appear in arms, imprisoning each other, and committing other enormities, to forward their *covetous* and *ambitious* purposes. Guibert, abbot of Nogent, in the diocess of Laon, wrote many excellent things, respecting the studies and duties of clergymen, the necessity of teaching both by word and example, and the subjects on which he ought to preach. He adds an idea, very surprising at that time, viz. that, as it is the duty of every preacher to lead a virtuous life, so it is the duty of *all christians who have attained to any knowledge of the holy scriptures, to preach the word of God.*

Honorius of Autun, a scholastic divine, wrote a very sensible treatise on Free-will, and Predestination. He defines the latter to be, " an eternal preparation of those who have done good or evil, to happiness or misery ; and affirms that it imposes no necessity of doing either ; because God predestinates to happiness or misery, only with respect to the merits of the person."

One Guigue, prior of Grenoble, taught " that recourse ought not to be had *to arms*, or to the *secular powers*, to maintain the temporal interests of the church, or to augment it's grandeur."

These I quote, out of several instances, to shew that common sense, and liberality of sentiment, were beginning to revive. Sorry, however, I am to add, that new absurdities also showed themselves. The term " Transubstantiation," was now first used by Peter de Celles, bishop of Chartres, and Stephen, bishop of Autun. Reter de Blois, archdeacon of Bath, soon after adopted it. His own words must be the safest vehicle of his ideas, on this subject, *if any such he had*. They are as follow: " In one single sacrament, *a deep abyss impenetrable to human reason ;* I mean, in the bread and wine, *transubstantiated* into the body and blood of Jesus Christ, by virtue of the heavenly words, ye see the accidents, which were therein, remaining without a subject: and, although the body of Jesus Christ be flesh, and not spirit, nevertheless it 'nourishes the soul, rather than the body. The same body is to be found in several places, and on divers altars, contrary to the nature of bodies, without ceasing to be in heaven : for though, by its nature, it can be only in one place, *after a circumscriptible manner*, yet it is in *many places, by its omnipotent virtue and energy*, and *after a spiritual manner.*" See here *consubstantiation* in embryo ! Many other instances of this kind might be quoted as the first-fruits of scholastic divinity, which was now introduced by the famous Peter Abelard, already mentioned ; Gilbert de Porree, bishop of Poitiers ; Peter Lombard, bishop of Paris ; Robert Pullus, archdeacon of Rochester ; Robert de Melun, bishop of Hereford, and some others. Peter Lombard's book of sentences was published, about the year 1160. It made a wonderful change in the *then* literary world. The *song* of *Solomon*, and the *revelations*, were no longer the theme of *love-sick divines*, and *dreaming mystagogues*. Dissertations on *the sentences* employed every pen of wrangling pedants, and supplied amusement to systematic fools. In fact, this same book of sentences contains the substance of all the absurdities, which have been written, or preached, on theological subjects, or systems, from that day to this. A few of the questions which he conjured up, and discussed, will be sufficient to give an idea of his whole work. " *Whether it may be said, that God, the Father, begat himself ; or whether it* OUGHT TO TO BE SAID, THAT HE BEGAT ANOTHER GOD ? *Whether it may be said, that the Father begat the Divine Essence, or the Divine Essence begat the Son ; or whether one essence produced another ; or whether the essence be neither produced, nor producing ? Whether the Father begat the Son, by necessity, or by his own will ? Whether the Father even endued with especial will and power to beget the son? Whether it may be said that the divine nature was born of the Virgin Mary? Whether Jesus Christ, as man, be a person or a thing?* Be ashamed and blush, ye modern mystagogues! Peter Lombard outran you so far, in the path of absurdity, that you will never overtake him.

Commentaries on the bible began to be written in the same style, and stuffed with useless questions and mystical subtleties. That of Rupert, an abbot, may be taken as a specimen of the whole. In treating of the holy Trinity and its works, he divides them into three parts: 1st, from the creation to the fall of Adam; 2d, From the fall to the passion of Christ; 3d, To the day of judgment. The first period he appropriates to the rule of the Father; the second to that of the Son; and the third to the holy Spirit. This system of divine superintendance, was revived in the fourteenth century, as we shall see afterwards, and greatly improved in wildness and absurdity.

Without farther details, I shall only observe, in general, that in this century, the schisms of the popes, and their contests with emperors and kings, which distracted the church, and produced numberless calamities to the people, in their effects, consolidated and extended the papal power. The popes established their Sovereignty in Rome, and their independence on the emperor; and usurped the right of conferring the Imperial crown. Most of the councils were called by the mandate of them, or their legates. Canons were enacted by their authority, the bishops merely concurring. They prohibited all sorts of people to profess divinity, or preach publicly, without a licence from the holy See, or the diocesan bishop, and anathematized all who presumed to maintain doctrines or practices, different from those of the church. —The clergy to be deposed—laics to be deliverd for punishment, to the secular judge. Appeals to Rome became universal, and were as universally complained of. Against several kinds of them, the third council of the Lateran had the hardihood to enact prohibitions. Dispensations, also, became so common and cheap, that every man of sense or goodness considered them as a baneful grievance. They not only set aside all discipline, but afforded patronage to every enormity.

Though many canons had formerly been enacted, forbidding the clergy to marry, under pain of penance, or degradation; yet their marriage was not declared null, nor divorce enjoined, before the second council of the Lateran, in the year 1139.

Universities began to be formed; among which, those of Paris and Bononia were the most famous; the former for divinity, and the latter for civil law. Bishops were obliged to have persons in their cathedrals, capable of teaching the arts and sciences; and the clergy became somewhat less ignorant and irregular.

Many new questions were introduced concerning the sacraments; and their celebration was reduced to an absurd and extravagant system. In baptism, amidst all the mummeries annexed to the original institution, triple dipping continued in use. The eucharist was usually administered in both kinds, during the whole of this century; though, in the beginning of it, some only dipped the bread in the wine; and, towards the end, some received only in one kind.

For the remission of sins, croisades and pilgrimages began to be substituted, in place of public penance. Monachism gained ground, both in popularity and power. Episcopal benediction of monks, which originated in the east, was now given in the west; and an express profession enjoined them. Monasteries were allowed to *receive*, but not to *demand*, money, from those whom they admitted. This distinction, however, they seem to have easily disposed of. Poor at first, they soon became rich. Riches begat pride and jealousy; and these soon generated quarrels. Some monasteries obtained, from the popes, exemption from episcopal jurisdiction; and some favorite abbots got permission to wear episcopal ornaments. Though monks were not allowed to administer the sacraments, and perform the other offices of curates; it is remarkable, that many were taken out of monasteries to be made bishops and cardinals; and equally so, that bishops, in the end of life, frequently retired into these solitary mansions, to conclude their days in *pious* exercises, and die in peace.

Military orders were multiplied, in this century, on account of the vast numbers who made pilgrimages. The first was the order of St. John of Jerusalem, or *Knights*

Hospitallers, instituted for the entertainment of pilgrims travelling to, and from, that city: the second, that of *Knights Templars*, to protect them on their journey: the third, *Knights of the Teutonic Order*, who were to perform both offices; and afterwards, *Knights of St. James*, and of *Calatrava*, for like purposes, in Spain.

On the whole, this age exhibits but a gloomy aspect. The best, which can be said of it, with all its improvements, either in the subjects or modes of study, is, that it is less dark and dismal than the two preceding.

In the thirteenth century, several revolutions took place, in Italy and the empire. In all which the popes were deeply concerned. The greater part of it was filled by wars between them and the emperors, or the kings of Sicily, as they hoped to annex that island, and the territory of Naples, to the papal domains.

In these contests, the pontiffs added the thunders of the church to the terrors of the sword; issued bulls of deposition against kings and emperors; and declared their subjects absolved from the obligation of oaths, and every tie of allegiance. These were little regarded, in general, and the kings of France, not only treated them with contempt, but exposed them to ridicule. However, partial interests, and civil broils, among the petty princes of Italy, and a common desire of lessening the Imperial power, were the cause of extending both the power and territory of the Roman See. Latterly, after many struggles, and a variety of changes, the house of Austria succeeded that of Suabia, and obtained peaceable possession of the German empire, in the person of Albert, son of Rodolphus, the first emperor of that family.

While the pontiffs were growing in power, the bishops encreasing their revenues, and the clergy, in general, multiplying their absurdities, and impositions, the people, in many places, began to turn their attention from their fooleries and mystical nonsense, to the only true source of religious knowledge, edification, and comfort. They got copies of the sacred books, and held private assemblies, where they read and expounded them, to each other. By these the eyes of their understandings were enlightened, and new prospects were opened before them. The gross misrepresentations of religion, in all its parts, which had so long imposed upon them, roused indignation against their authors, and an ardent zeal for truth and virtue. In the diocess of Metz, in France, they preached publicly even against the priests, and their adherents became so numerous, that the church was a-alarmed, and Pope Innocent 3d drew his pen to write them down. This failing, he attacked them afterwards with more formidable weapons, as we shall have occasion to observe.

The number of these new teachers, and the success of their labors, may be easily estimated, by the measures adopted by popes, and sanctioned by councils, in order to suppress them. As the spiritual power had become contemptible, and even excommunication with all its penalties was treated with ridicule. Innocent, who had forbidden the use of force or violence to drive the Jews to the baptismal font, concurred in opinion with the *holy* order of bishops, that both should be used against all whom they were pleased to call *Heretics.* The measure was no sooner approved than executed. Nor was it, as formerly, in a few instances, confined to individuals. *A holy war, for the extirpation of the whole, was proclaimed, and* PREACHED. But as war could only reach public professors, without affecting *secret assemblies,* more than war was necessary. To complete the plan, therefore, Innocent instituted a *tribunal,* till then unknown and unheard of, and a band of HOLY SPIES, CATCHPOLLS, and public ACCUSERS, whose office it was to detect, lay hold of, and draw up informations against all heretics. This tribunal was called the " HOLY INQUISITION ;" and the new erected orders of Dominican and Franciscan friars were turned out among the people to seize victims, and drag them to the altar of frantic superstition, and *priestly* vengeance. At first, the office of the holy inquisitors, was only that of *spies, informers,* and *accusers ;* the power of condemning the accused, rested with the ordinary judges. However, the inquisitors soon obtained a power of sitting in judgment conjunctly with the bishops, in trials of heretics ; and the secular power retained the solitary honor of being *executioner* to the court. This tribunal was first established in Languedoc, against the Albigenses, and Waldenses ; and soon extended its influence over France, Spain, and Italy. In France it was soon exploded, and Germany never admitted it.

This institution, though *unreasonable, inhuman, antichristian,* and *diabolical,* may be palliated by the shadow of consistency. However liberality and common sense may reprobate the idea of depriving men of property, liberty, or life, for matter of mere opinion, form, or ceremony, it must be admitted that the opinions, forms, and ceremonies which were the objects of its inquest and arms, were merely religious; and that these come properly under the cognizance and correction of religious ministers. The error and the evil, therefore, consisted not in the inquest, but, where the *supposed* guilt was found, in the punishment adjudged, and the instruments and agents, by which it was inflicted. Had the HOLY fathers confined themselves, in such cases, to the instruments and agents, prescribed by reason, the BIBLE, and a regard to the souls of men—had they hewed down the *supposed* errors, superstitions, and impieties, which they condemned, with " the sword of the spirit, which is the word of God," instead of consigning to beggary, imprisonment, exile, or death, *by the subserviency of the civil power,* those who wandered, or were led astray in religion's path—had they reasoned to enlighten, and rebuked to reform, instead of precluding all possibility of either by the extinction of life—succeeding generations would have honored them as MEN, and blessed them as MEN OF GOD. However, this was not the case. Hence, *the mention of their name inspires horror, and their memory is accursed !* Though, *in their modesty,* they only framed the accusation, and pronounced the sentence, leaving the execution to the civil power. If this be the fact—and that it is so, the nations know—what feelings would they have excited ; and where would language have been found to express them, had they proceeded to the enormities to be committed in future ages ! I shudder, in looking forward to a day, not far distant, when the ministers of a church, calling itself reformed, and boasting of its liberality, indifferent to religious principle, religious form, and religion's spirit, shall press themselves on kings as VOLUNTEER INQUISITORS OF STATE—when, after, *pompously,* profanely, and blasphemously, holding up " their faithful exertions as an ATONEMENT for their deluded brethren," they shall pledge themselves " to make strict enquiry into the political conduct of their delinquent members"—when the general body shall " strictly enjoin their several subordinate judicatories, to institute a so-LEMN inquiry into the political conduct and conversation of their respective members and probationers, and to make a faithful report of their procedure under penalty of severe censure"—when, in contempt of decency and the existing government, they shall continue to punish, by every mean in their power, those whom the lenity of the state has pardoned, or its justice pronounced innocent by overt acts—acts more expressive than any words —and, when they shall conclude their blasphemies, inquests, and persecutions, with the worse than senseless prayer, that " *the king of kings may convert their follies, crimes and miseries, into instruments of wisdom, piety, and happiness, both now and for ever!*" Hue! miseranda dies!! Pastores hue! exurandi!!!

The councils of this age were numerous, and their sittings are marked with some circumstances favorable to their character; yet these are more than counterbalanced by others of a different complexion, and more in number. The fourth council of the Lateran, in 1215, confirmed and extended a decree of Alexander 3d, as follows; " There shall be, in all cathedral churches, a master, to teach *gratis* the clergy of those churches, and the *other poor scholars*; in other churches there shall be the master of a grammar school; and, in the metropolitan churches, besides such master, a *divine to teach the priests and other ecclesiastics*, the holy scriptures, and what relates to the cure of souls." In 1231, the council of Chateau enacted, that " those who received benefices with cure of souls, shall understand the vulgar language of the country." The utility of these institutions must be obvious; though the necessity of the latter may not at first sight appear. But, let it be observed, that the nations of Europe had not then the same intercourse as now, by which they could acquire even an imperfect knowledge of the languages of each other—that to the richer benefices, men were sent from one kingdom into another—and from Italy, in particular, into every country subject to the See of Rome. From this, the necessity of the canon must be evident and undeniable. Nay, even in more enlightened times, and where no such circumstances exist, the necessity of such canon is too, too obvious. Would to learning and decency! it were less so even now, or likely to be so. Even within the last half century there existed a clerical body, as I am told, which, if counted off by fives, *at random*, would afford one, in each lot, who could neither write, read, speak, nor spell, *correctly*, his native tongue.

But let the necessity or usefulness of such regulations be obvious as possible; that usefulness was checked, by counter-canons, as soon as its effects appeared. Flimsy as the education was, it excited inquiry; inquiry led to new ideas; these ideas to the exposure of prevailing ignorance, superstition, priestcraft, and clerical usurpation; and this exposure to the establishment of the *holy inquisition*. No sooner was this tribunal erected by Innocent, than councils gave it their solemn sanction, and extended its jurisdiction. One, assembled at Narbonne, in 1227, enacted, not only, "that there shall be, *in every parish*, inquisitors after heretics," but that they shall be excluded from all places of trust;" and that "lords, governors, judges, and other officers shall expel them." Two years afterwards, the council of Toulouse confirmed these canons, and enforced them by severe penalties. No less than forty-five canons were enacted, in which the inquisitors are bound by oath to execute their office with zeal; lords are enjoined to search out heretics, and destroy their places of resort, under penalty of losing their estates; houses where they are found, are to be pulled down, and the ground confiscated; bailiffs, who do not strictly aid the pious purpose, are condemned to the loss of office and estate; recanting heretics are to be shut up in walled places, lest they should corrupt others; and all men above fourteen years of age, and women above twelve, are obliged to abjure all kinds of heresy, to make a profession of the faith of Rome, and to persecute heretics. Heretics are forbidden to come near the sick; and even those suspected of heresy, are prohibited the practice of physic.

One would think that these canons, with the penalties annexed, were enough, in all conscience, to stifle inquiry, preclude knowledge, render heresy impossible, and secure the clergy in the quiet possession of their *creeds, revenues, respectability, and influence.*

However, a following canon shows that they did not think themselves secure, *while the bible was in the hands of the people.* It shows also, the object of their *schools,* and the extent of the education afforded in their cathedrals. We have already seen that this education in *divinity* and the *knowledge of the holy scriptures,* was intended for the *priests* of the respective churches, and the other *prior scholars.* It should be recollected also, that the councils in which the erection of schools was injoined, as observed on a former occasion, were more properly parliaments, in which princes and temporal lords had great influence. That the benefit was never designed, *by the clergy,* to extend to the people at large, is evident from the canon alluded to. It peremptorily prohibits their having *the old or new testaments* in their possession, or even a *prayer-book,* or *psalter,* in the *vulgar tongue.* The synod of Arles, in 1233, went farther than any of the preceding. It not only condemned heretics to perpetual imprisonment, and delivered the obstinate to the civil power, *to be farther dealt with;* but ordered the bodies and bones of those, whose heresy should be discovered after their death, to be dug up; so that even the grave, "the house of rest for all flesh," was no security against the frantic rage of vengeful ecclesiastics. Be it observed, that this last council was only provincial, and that it does not appear to have contained one layman. Perhaps the ELDERS were excluded, lest they should oppose these decrees of darkness, persecution, and violence to the dead.

Four years after this, Cardinal Otho, legate, being invited to England, by Henry 3d, held a council in London. Its canons related merely to discipline. It does not appear that either heresy or inquisition was even mentioned. Otho is said to have conducted himself with great moderation; yet the nobles were much offended at the great respect shown him by the king.

The king of Scotland behaved very differently. He would not permit the legate to enter his kingdom; but told him "that he had no occasion for him; that all was well enough in his realm; that his people had never seen a legate there; nor would he suffer any; and that he would do well not to expose himself by coming among them, as they were rude and uncivilized, and might, perhaps, use him ill."

Through the remaining councils of this age, little

appears but canons, concerning discipline, the revenues and jurisdiction of the church, the reformation and habits of the clergy, concubinage and the like.

The disputes between the university of Paris and the Dominican friars, who infringed on their privileges, and were patronized by the pontiffs, are of little importance in a religious point of view. They serve only to show the rivalry between the parties, and the anxiety of the popes to harass and humble a body, which uniformly opposed their attempts at temporal sovereignty in France. Nor are the controversies about a book, entitled " *the Eternal Gospel*," and the opinions of au abbot, called Joachim, more useful or interesting.

From the middle of this century, several sects, and half-formed systems, present themselves, as well as individuals, partly characterized by wildness and extravagance, and partly by honest zeal, sound sense, and primitive simplicity.

The most important of these sects, were the simple and virtuous Waldenses and Albigenses. The former took their name from Peter Valdo, a rich merchant of Lyons. The sudden death of a friend so affected his mind, that he *literally* abandoned the world, gave all his goods to the poor, and determined to restore what he deemed, the primitive and apostolical mode of life. His simplicity, devotion, and disinterestedness, soon procured him many followers, who copied his example. From their voluntary poverty, they were also called, " the poor of Lyons ;" and from the name of their city, " Leontines." Valdo being a man of learning, explained the New Testament, in the vulgar tongue, and instructed them so well, otherwise, that many of them soon began to preach. At first, however, they showed no design of establishing a new sect; but only of introducing an humble, sober, and pious life. But ecclesiastics began to declaim, and popes to issue damnatory bulls against them; the king of Arragon condemned, and bishops proscribed them. This irritated their passions and stimulated to inquiry. With the word of God, as their light, they could not avoid seeing the errors, absurdities, irregularities, and impositions of the clergy, and the irremovable inconsistency between the *religion* of the *church*, and the *religion of the bible*. Thus, irritated and enlightened, they rejected the authority of the bishops; declaimed against the inferior orders; declared that their sins annulled their services; preached against all manner of swearing, and the taking away of a human life, on any account whatever; and rejected the doctrines of the church, about worshipping saints and relicks, about indulgences and ceremonies, the sacraments, *as then prostituted*, and purgatory.

As enemies cannot be supposed to flatter, I shall extract a slight sketch of these people from the picture drawn by the pencil of an enemy.

" In the first place," says Raynerius, " they say that the church of Rome, is a church of wicked men, and not the church of Christ; but has ceased to be so, since the time of St. Sylvester, when the POISON OF TEMPORALITIES crept into it—that they are the true church of Christ, because they follow the Doctrine of Christ and his apostles, *in word and action*; and the truly poor in spirit, because they suffer persecution for the sake of righteousness and the faith—and that the church of Rome is the harlot, mentioned in the revelation, on account of her superfluous ornaments—that the pope is the *author of all errors*; the prelates, *scribes*; and the monks *pharisees*—that the pope and bishops are murderers, because of the wars which they occasion—that, in matters of religion, *God only should be obeyed*—that the titles of prelate, pope, and bishop, ought to be rejected —that ecclesiastical benefices and privileges are null and void—that the privileges of curates are human inventions, and the rules of monks, pharisaical traditions.—They denied that the washing of infants, the surety of sponsors, unctions, benedictions, and exorcisms, in baptism, were of any use. They rejected the sacrament of confirmation. They maintained that a wicked priest could neither *consecrate* nor *transubstantiate*, in the eucharist; and that a common table was as fit for the purpose as an altar. They asserted that the mass was nothing, because the apostles *never* said it, and the priests, *only for their own interest*; and that it was better to confess to a good laic, than to a bad priest—that the prayers of a wicked priest are of no value; and extreme unction, a solemn foolery—that *scripture is the only rule of faith*—that the doctrines of Christ and his apostles are sufficient to make wise to salvation—that they have no mystical meaning; and that the traditions of the church are silly fables. They despised and rejected the dedication, benediction, and consecration of wax tapers, boughs, chrism, fire, lying-in women, pilgrims, churches, altars, and all other customs of the church, *not authorised by the gospel.* They condemned images, denied purgatory, ridiculed masses for the dead, and pronounced the invocation of saints and angels an impious mockery."

From the view here given of these people, no cause of persecution can present itself, except to the eye of a superstitious people, whose minds were poisoned by an ignorant, interested, and merciless priesthood. Many other sects arose, and became numerous in this century, *in spite of the inquisition,* both in France and Spain. A remnant of the Waldenses outlived their many persecutions, till, in the year 1630, they united with the Calvinists.

The sect of the Albigenses, which was very numerous, seems, in some measure, to have been composed of all the preceding. It spread over Languedoc, Provence, Dauphine, and Arragon; and was patronized by Raymond, count of Toulouse. Innocent the third used every mean to extirpate them, by exciting, both the clergy and civil powers against them; but to little effect, for a long time. The vices of the clergy, as all the historians of the time agree, did more in their favor, than all the powers and persecutions of the world could undo. To this fact, a single circumstance gives unbounded credit, and clothes with clerical honor the character of those worthy votaries of virtue and religion. This is the declaration of Didarus, bishop of Osma, in an assembly of *bishops, abbots,* and *monks,* holden in 1207, to devise means of *converting* these heretics. " Ye must lay aside," says he, " your *covetousness, pride, pomp, and magnificence, embrace the example of Jesus Christ, and demonstrate your faith, not only by your words, but by your actions, if ye would serve the souls of those, whom these heretics have deceived by a semblanc of piety and virtue.*" To strengthen his opinion, which was seemingly approved, he dismissed his pompous equipage, and became a zealous preacher; and a few others followed his laudable example: but, alas! the pious effort was too late and limited. *Clerical wickedness* had inflicted a wound too deep for *partial clerical reformation*, even if real, to cure. But, even its reality, partial as it was, was suspected. Hence, the effect was totally lost. Persecution was again resorted to the inquisitors let loose—and a *holy war, under the auspices of the clergy*, preached and practised, against those honest, brave, and religious people. Princes, counts, barons, and all their blood-hounds took the field: popes issued the thunders of the church: prelates played off its artillery: and synods sanctioned the whole *in the name of the holy trinity!* Conflagration succeeded conflagration, and massacre followed massacre, wherever their arms prevailed, till the strength of the people of God was overpowered, and their voice silenced; but blessed—ever blessed be his name! their *spirit was not extinguished*, though the conditions imposed upon them, *by their holy conquerors*, were severe and tyrannical, as ever disgraced the annals, even *of the clergy*.

In Italy and the Empire, also, different sects appeared about this time. Of their particular opinions, a detail would not be interesting. Most of them showed a great deal of good sense, but debased by an equal proportion of extravagance and folly, as may be expected, from the ignorance of the times, and the impertinences and depravity of their clergy, whose superstitions had perverted their understanding, and whose example had corrupted their hearts. Among these the *whippers* appear most conspicuous. They had taken up an idea equally wild and impious, that the mercy of God to their souls, was to be obtained by the voluntary infliction of pains on their bodies; and that thirty-four successive days of self whipping secured the pardon of all sins. Hence, multitudes of men of all ages and qualities, preceded by priests were seen in public processions, two and two, half-naked, and belabouring themselves with scourges, till their bodies were streaming with blood. Women and maids contented themselves with exercising this *pious* discipline, *privately*, at home. Then also, popes, princes, prelates, and doctors (the title of doctor now began to supercede that of *saint*) remonstrated against, persecuted, and anathematized them. In fact, at this period differed from the customs of the church, or interfered with the clergy in their eager pursuit of wealth, or ambitious efforts to obtain a higher CLASS, exposed the author to persecution on earth, and, *if we believe the reverend and holy fathers, to the pains of hell.* At least, so far as the clergy had, either *power,* or the *ear of men in power,* every thing, *in their way,* was levelled : and, if we may judge by recent facts, wherever the clergy become *parasites* of government, *habitual suppliant* for the *offals* of the *treasury,* or the *idolaters of upstart ministers,* and *apostate courtiers,* the same will be the case for ever. The interests of the christian people, the sentiments of justice and humanity, and the independence of religion and conscience will be sacrificed together, before the shrine of covetousness and ambition.—Nay, *before the prince of darkness himself,* if he hold out BOUNTY in the one hand, and CLASSIFICATION in the other.

As this century presents great efforts of the people to restore learning, and acquire knowledge ; it presents efforts equally great to keep the former in chains, and suppress the latter. We have already seen that, with this view, the people were deprived of the use of the bible, or even of a prayer-book in a known tongue. To this a council of the clergy, at Paris, added the condemnation of the writings of Aristotle, newly imported from Constantinople, and translated into Latin ; ordered them to be burned, and forbade the study of them, *under pain of excommunication:* and the legate of his holiness confirmed the decree of darkness. God of Light ! shall those whom thou hast appointed to be " *the lights of the world,*" continue, for ever, *extinguishers of the light of knowledge.* Shall they, who ought to be " the salt of the earth," to preserve it from corruption, be an eternal pool of mental rottenness, whose streams shall pollute , and exhalations poison the souls of men ? Prevent it, O God !—Gracious God prevent it !

The reduction of the universities and accademies, founded in the preceeding century, to a regular form, and the establishment of a few others, hold out a promising appearance ; yet, during this century, they affected little. At first, these seminaries consisted, only, of *masters and scholars.* There were no forms of conferring degrees. *Ca-*

alone—were attended to. Afterwards, several degrees were instituted and times of study prescribed for their attainment. Gregory 9th, who succeeded to the papal chair, in 1227 first instituted the degrees of " *bachelor, licentiate, and master or doctor.*" The bachelors taught publicly, gave explications of the holy scripture, and wrote treatises on Peter Lombard's famous " book of sentences." These gave rise to numberless *wise, learned, and unintelligible,* disputations in which the *doctors* presided as *moderators.* Various disputes arose, between the universities and the clergy, about the right of conferring degrees; but, finally, it was vested in the universities. The first divinity schools were in the cloyster of Notredame, at St. Genevieve, and St. Victor. Several others soon followed. About the middle of the century, there were three divinity professorships at Notredame, seven among the secular doctors, and two of the Dominican friars. The other orders of monks soon added to the number. The sciences and philosophy, *such as they then were,* were taught, by many masters, in several schools. The chief of these masters was called " head of the school;" and held an office like that of our " rectors of universities."

The title of " bachelor" seems oddly accounted for, by some historians. As they taught the public schools, they are said to have been called " bacillarii," and " bacularii," from " bacilla," a small stick, or " baculus" a cudgel; because they were admitted to their degree, by giving them a slender stick, in allusion to novices in the militia, who first exercised with sticks, before they were allowed the use of arms. Admitting the general idea, is it not more probable, as *flogging* had become fashionable, that giving them the *bacilla,* or *baculus,* was a rite expressive of their power, where application to the ear was ineffectual, to try experiments upon the buttocks—a power exercised, with few exceptions, from the days of the Orbilii of ancient Rome, to those of the Brutii of modern Ullin? however, a more pleasing idea presents itself, and seems to have been afterwards adopted. The bachelor's degree was the first step towards the summit of academic honors, of which the laurel was the emblem. Hence, the word " baccalaurei'" not " bacillarii, has been used; and if not more proper, is certainly more honorable. Instead of presenting our " bachelors" as "licensed floggers," it recommends them as qualified to teach, because their own literary attainments had procured them their degree—their "laurel of science."

The election of bishops continued in the chapters, and of abbots and abbesses, in their respective societies, thro' Italy, France, England and Germany; tho' every art, and every effort, was used by the popes, to engross them entirely; and, finally, the publication of the Decretals rendered the papal power absolute and unlimited, by bringing processes innumerable before the court of Rome. The distinction between benefices with the cure of souls, and simple benefices was introduced. Pluralities became common; and the jurisdiction, privileges, and immunities of the clergy were stretched to the utmost. Hence, their insolence became unbounded; their licentiousness bade defiance to all decency, and their covetousness was insatiable. In the pursuit of revenues they trampled religion under-foot, insulted the persons of men, and made traffic of their souls. The great body of the clergy, however, still found obstacles to retard them in their race towards the temple of mammon. Princes taxed them, for the exigency of states; and popes for croisades, to employ the attention, withdraw the forces, and lessen the power, of princes, that the impediments to the increase of their own might be diminished. The institution, and progress of the mendicant-friars, though intended by Innocent the 3d to rival and counteract the poverty and virtue of the Waldenses, operated more powerful against the interests, of the clergy, by presenting a second contract to their irregularities, excesses, and shameless extortions. The contests between the parties were long and violent. Councils interfered, and uniformly supported the claims of the clergy; while popes decreed, on one side, or the other, as circumstances varied. The result of these contests was highly favourable to the restoration of knowledge and religious truth. It opened the eyes of multitudes to the weakness, and worthlessness of the parties, kindled a generous indignation, and extended inquiry.

Besides the mendicants, several other orders took their rise in this century. The Minor, or Franciscan Friars; the hermits of St. Augustine; the Order of the Holy Trinity, or Redemption of Captives; that of St. Mary of Mercy; of Celestines; and of the Vally of

Scholars; sprung up in the West; and that of Carmil-
ites was imported from Palestine. Over all these the
Mendicants, who took the name of Dominicans, from
their founder, acquired a pre-eminence, which they long
retained, by the zeal with which they preached, over all
the christian world, against the Waldenses, Albigenses,
and all who opposed, or endeavoured to reform established error, absurdity, superstition and sin.

The writings of this age are more numerous than valuable; though, on several subjects, many sensible things
appeared. William, bishop of Paris, and Robert Gros-
tede, bishop of Lincoln, wrote with good sense, and
great zeal, against pluralities, and the collation of benefices on minors, and persons grossly ignorant, or immoral. The boldness of the latter, in refusing to appoint
a young Italian, nephew to the pope, to a canonry in
Lincoln, gave great offence to Innocent 4th, and drew
from him a torrent of folly, impertinence, and scurrility,
which may be taken as a sample of the spirit and manners of the times, as well as of popes. "What an old
doating, impertinent fellow is this," exclaimed he,
"who dares, thus impudently, to call my conduct in
question! By *St. Peter and St. Paul*, were it not my respect for his ingenuity, I would make him a talk, astonishment, and example to all the world, and present him
as a prodigy. Is not his master, the king of England,
who, at our nod, can bury him in a dungeon, and cover
him with infamy, our VASSAL, or rather our SLAVE!!!"
Let one other circumstance suffice to convince us of the
short progress of literature and science in this age. A-
mong the few, who had any pretensions to either, Roger
Bacon held, and ever will hold, a conspicuous place.
Yet the principal, immediate effects of his wonderful discoveries, in mathematics, physics, and chymistry, were
repeated charges of his being a conjuror, his condemnation, as such, by the general of his order, in 1278, and
his imprisonment, the year following, by order of the
Pope, Nicholas 4th.

The theological writings of this century are of little
value. Lombard's sentences were the only system of divinity attended to, or taught: and they were rendered
more perplexed and senseless, by an abuse of Aristotle's
philosophy, ill understood, and worse applied. In the

few commentaries on the holy scripture, which this age produced, little is to be found, except quibbles, allegory, and mysticism. Little better can be said of works on piety; and the writers, on the multiplied and exaggerated ceremonies of the church, have puzzled themselves to discover *mystical* reasons for them all. History was neglected, only as it related to croisades, pilgrimages, and lives of saints. And multitudes of commentaries, upon Aristotle's philosophy, served only to darken, debase, and corrupt it. The pulpit contributed as little as the pen, to the recovery and extension of useful knowledge. The word of God was tainted with a mixture of the jargon of the schools. Sermons consisted of divisions and sub-divisions, without either meaning or use, distinctions without difference, mean comparisons, forced antitheses, distorted figures, and foreign allegories. Morality was neglected, or, at lest, little attended to: and scripture was introduced, merely to show the taste or abilities of the sermonist, in twisting or bending it to his own porpose; and making it speak, what, the supreme intelligence, by which it was dictated, never intended.

I have, already taken notice that, about this time, the rage of *saintship* began to subside before the vanity of science, *yet in infancy*. The first voice of the latter, when she attained the use of speech, excited such wonder in the ignorant, love in those who had taste to distinguish her opening charms, and astonishment in simpletons, that no terms were deemed too dignified, or tender, to characterize the different doctors of the time. Hence, the world rung with the fame of *admirable doctors, angelical doctors, seraphic doctors, solemn, solid, subtle,* and *singular doctors.* There were also *profound doctors, pragmatical doctors,* and *golden doctors.* In a word, had we not called in *size* and *color,* and some other circumstances, merely adventitious, to furnish names and epithets, language was so exhausted, that doctors of later ages might have passed undefined, and undenominated.

In respect to the councils of this age, we have noticed only those canons, which exhibit the zeal of the clergy in suppressing knowledge, and persecuting, under the writing, opposed the established ignorance, superstition, and idolatry of the church. Canons, however, securing the revenues of the clergy, now become excessive, prohibiting their multiplied extortions, and imposing restraints on their unbridled licentiousness, were much more numerous. Between the first and second classes of these canons, there is an apparent inconsistency. However it is only apparent. The revenues of the higher classes, and all their imposts were to be secured and extended by the one; the rapacity and extortions of the lower, stimulated by necessity, were the objects of the latter. Thus, while the whole body were hunting after riches, the best endowed were straining every nerve to secure to themselves and their connexions, every thing lucrative, not only within their reach, but within their view. This shameless conduct, though oppressive for a time, had the happiest effects. It opened the eyes of the people, more and more, to the worthlessness of their mercenary clergy, alienated their affections, excited a generous indignation, and roused that sense of *religious rights*, the exercise of which restored to a great portion of Europe the enjoyment of *religious liberty*, about two hundred years afterwards.

As, from this period, the ecclesiastical scene exhibits a new drapery, new actors, and new events, all deeply interesting to a religious and benevolent mind, I shall here pause, and allow my reader to reflect on what I have fairly, though tenderly laid before him. May he reflect with judgment, imbibe wisdom with humility, and improve the lessons, which the few preceding pages teach, with honest zeal and christian fortitude! The moment calls for *reflexion, wisdom, zeal,* and *fortitude*. It calls for *them all*, and they ought not to be separated. I trust they never will be separated. Whether, and how far this confidence will be justified, by approaching events, a short time will show. That it may be universally justified—*that religion pure and unadulterated, may ever be preserved where it is; that it may be successfully planted and propagated, where yet it has not appeared— that it may be speedily and effectually restored wherever it is lost, or going to decay—till the knowledge of its principles shall enlighten every understanding, its spirit purify every*

*heart, its precepts regulate every action, and its prospects
rejoice every spirit among men, is the fervent prayer of my
heart!* Were I to add more of my own to what I have
copied, and sometimes only abridged, I would only say,
that every age, as I proceeded, confirmed me more and
more in the opinion, which my feelings obliged me,
more than once, to express, that the clergy, from the
earliest ages, wherever they have attached themselves to
the riches and honors of the world, have injured the
cause of knowledge and religion, and uniformly obstruct-
ed the restoration of both, on their genuine principles.
If I have, in the warmth of my heart, concluded rashly,
or spoken with freedom void of flattery, I wish, *most
earnestly,* to be informed and corrected *with the same freedom.* But let my correctors *read, again and again,* before they let loose their *whetted* tongues, dip their pens
in gall, or put their hands to the birch. Facts are stubborn *things :* and, I am fully convinced, that the uniform series of facts, from the days of Moses to the present moment, must be sweated down to shadowy fictions,
or resolved into airy dreams, before a lash of the tongue,
a drop of the gall, or a stroke of the birch, can fall on
me. Besides, *I believe the Bible!* I believe that *its
word of prophecy is sure and steadfast!* And, that events
will prove it to be *yea!* and *amen.* And, of consequence, I must believe, that the prophecies, already quoted, concerning the ignorance, covetousness, rapacity,
ambition, deceit, vain wranglings, proud boastings, calumnies, envies, contempt of honest men, sacrifice of religion to filthy lucre, or "following the way of Balaam
for *the wages of unrighteousness,*" uniformly have been,
now are, and hereafter will be, in a state of completion,
till the whole shall be fulfilled; and God, in his goodness, shall raise up a new, learned, wise, pure and dis-
interested order of ministers, which, like constellations
in a new heaven, shall illuminate the earth by their knowledge, and renew it by their example.

End of the first Patch.

9 781535 811439